The Unconscious Script

A Guide to Your Soul's Patterns and The Evolution of Consciousness

ANGELA LANCASTER

Copyright © 2025 Angela Lancaster

ISBN: 979-8-218-88823-7

Published by Alchemist of Paradox

All rights reserved.

Dedication

To Michael and Kaylee

Thank you for loving me through my worst and my becoming.
Your love met me where I was, not where I pretended to be.
You taught me what unconditional love feels like — not as an idea,
but as a lived truth. Loving you became the catalyst that required my growth,
and through that love, my soul could finally feel whole. I love you eternally

To Ashley, Austin, and Andrew

Thank you for choosing me to be your mom,
for the sacred time your souls allowed me to participate in,
for the lessons, the mirrors, and the love
that continues to echo through lifetimes.
I carry you with me in every chapter,
in every breath of this work.
I love you all eternally

The Source

the quiet consciousness beneath every collapse, the voice that
whispered through the void, the divinity that refused to disappear
even when every identity fell away. You wrote this book through me.
You carried me into the life I was meant to live.
You are the truth I will never lose again.

TABLE OF CONTENTS

    Acknowledgments

1. Introduction
2. The Unconscious Script   Pg 1
3. Soul Patterns   Pg 23
4. Evolutionary Intent   Pg 48
5. Archetypal Intentions   Pg 55
6. The Planets   Pg 124
7. Emotional Patterns   Pg 143
8. Mirrors   Pg 153
9. Putting it All Together   Pg 165

ACKNOWLEDGMENTS

To Jeffrey Wolf Green
Thank you for bringing Evolutionary Astrology into this world. Your teachings ignited my passion, shaped my understanding, and opened the door to the spiritual language through which this book was born. Your work lives on in every soul these words will reach.

To the loves, losses, rejections, and closed doors that redirected my life
Thank you for being my teachers

To my younger self — Thank you for surviving long enough to meet the woman who could finally answer.

To the readers —
The ones who feel too deeply, think too intricately,
break too easily, and rebuild too fiercely
this book is for you.
May you see yourself in these pages
and remember the truth you were born with.

1 INTRODUCTION

From a young age, I was captivated by the unseen layers of human experience—the subtle movements of thought, the patterns of behavior, the invisible threads that pull people into loops of pain they can't name. While other children were navigating friendships and hobbies, I sat alone in my room with my eyes closed, asking questions far too existential for someone who hadn't yet turned ten: "Who would I be if I wasn't me?" It wasn't a game. It was an inquiry. A portal. Every time I asked, I encountered the same vast and terrifying silence. The void. That space haunted me. But it also drew me in.

Even then, something in me recognized that the darkness wasn't empty—it was alive. It was the beginning of an initiation shaped by the archetypal forces of Saturn, Neptune, Uranus and Pluto. Structure. Illusion. Liberation. Death. Discipline. Dream. Rebel. Transformation. My adolescence, my twenties, and even my early thirties were characterized by a strange emotional repetition. Pain that felt familiar but couldn't be traced. Patterns that echoed something ancient yet unspoken. I felt like a character in a play I had never auditioned for, saying lines I didn't remember choosing.

Eventually, the suffering became impossible to ignore. By my mid-thirties, after years of cycling through the same wounds—unprocessed grief, and a deep, unnamed emptiness—I turned toward astrology, toward the unconscious, toward anything that could offer clarity. It helped me understand my childhood, my nervous system, and the psychological architecture of my trauma. But as helpful as it was, it only took me so far. Because even when I understood my patterns, I still couldn't change them. So the core question remained: Why? Why do certain wounds persist even after we "heal" them? Why do we keep recreating stories that destroy what we love? Why can insight illuminate—but not liberate?

That question followed me into the most destabilizing season of my life. My marriage cracked open and reformed itself more times than I could count. Everything I had built dissolved beneath my feet. And underneath it all, the void remained. Not as emptiness—but as potential. A sacred waiting room. That's when I stopped looking outward—for approval, for frameworks, for textbook solutions—and instead turned toward the archetypal, the spiritual, the ancestral, and the shadow. I began what I now call real healing—not because it was beautiful or efficient, but because it required me to become someone new.

I had always needed to understand—not just what happened, but why. Not just the psychological mechanism, but the metaphysical architecture beneath it. The mechanics of the psyche weren't enough. I wanted to understand why cycles repeat across generations, why certain souls incarnate into certain families, and how the invisible universe shapes the visible one. Traditional psychology gave me language. But not the whole picture. I didn't just want to understand behavior. I wanted to understand the architecture of the soul.

It was astrology that finally gave me the keys. The first time I read the works of Jeffrey Wolf Green, Alan Oken, and Alice Bailey, something ancient in me recognized the truth. Their synthesis of astrology, psychology, and esoteric spirituality felt like a native language I had forgotten. It wasn't about horoscopes or personality—it was about karmic threads, incarnational purpose, soul evolution, and the larger cosmic story we are each living out.

But even with their brilliance, I struggled. I couldn't apply it cleanly to my life. I needed something more specific, more lived, more embodied. And that is why this book exists. This book is the map I wished I had— a guide to understanding the patterns we inherited, the illusions we were born into, the structures we came to dismantle, and the God within we came to remember. If you are holding this book, you already know: Your life was never random.

2 THE UNCONSCIOUS SCRIPT

There is the story you tell yourself about who you are, and then there is the story your soul has been repeating long before you were born. Most people believe they are living consciously—making choices, building relationships, choosing partners, choosing careers, choosing reactions. Yet beneath every decision lies a far older intelligence: a subterranean narrative shaped by past lives, emotional memory, karmic patterns, unhealed wounds, and evolutionary intentions that have very little to do with the logic your current personality believes it operates from.

This narrative—the entire ecosystem of instinct, reaction, attraction, avoidance, desire, fear, and compulsion—is what I call The Unconscious Script. It is not metaphorical. It is not symbolic. It is literal in the psychological, emotional, and karmic sense. The Unconscious Script is the inherited choreography of the soul. And whether you know it or not, you are performing it every day. Most people think they are "failing" to change their lives because they lack motivation, discipline, clarity, or healing. But the deeper reality is this: You cannot outperform a script you have not yet made conscious.

What the Unconscious Script Really Is
The unconscious script is the story you've been living without ever remembering the souls intent to live it. It is the quiet architecture beneath your choices, your reactions, your desires, your collapses, and your longing for a life you can't quite name. It's not a belief. Not a memory. Not even a wound. It's the choreography your soul learned before you arrived — the rhythm you've been moving to long before you knew life had rhythm at all.

THE UNCONSCIOUS SCRIPT

Most people meet their unconscious script the same way: through repetition. The same argument, the same heartbreak, the same ending disguised as a new beginning. You keep walking into familiar emotional rooms, wondering how you got there again. You assume it's your fault, or your trauma, or your personality. But these moments are not accidents — they're the script trying to get your attention. The script forms from a mixture of your earliest environments, your nervous system's survival codes, the archetypal intentions in your chart, and the emotional memory your soul carried into this lifetime. It speaks in impulses, not logic. It whispers in sensations, not words. It emerges in the exact moment you lose control of the storyline — the moment your reactions seem to move faster than your awareness.

The mind thinks it's directing your life, but the script is directing your patterns. And until you can recognize its language, you'll keep mistaking the script for fate. At its core, the unconscious script is trying to preserve you. That's the painful irony. Every pattern that devastates you was originally created to protect you. The shutting down, the pleasing, the avoiding, the running, the clinging, the collapsing — these were choices made by an earlier self who believed survival depended on them. You're not broken. You're patterned. And patterns always repeat until they meet consciousness.

But consciousness isn't the same as insight. You can understand your childhood and still repeat its consequences. You can study astrology and still sabotage the destiny it reveals. You can speak the language of healing and still feel trapped inside the same emotional loop. Why? Because the script doesn't shift when you analyze it. It shifts when you *recognize it as something separate from who you are*. A pattern loses power the moment you see it as a pattern — not a personality. Not a flaw. Not a destiny.

Your chart describes this architecture with uncanny precision: the moon revealing emotional memory, Saturn revealing the karmic lesson, Pluto the souls' desires, the Nodes the tension between past and becoming. But even astrology can only point. You must feel the script in your body to rewrite it. The unconscious script isn't your enemy. It's the map of where you've been — and the doorway to who you're becoming. Once you learn its language, the repetition softens. The reactions slow. The pattern loosens. You stop living inside a story written by fear and begin writing one shaped by consciousness. And that is the moment your real life begins.

The Foundational Patterns
The Unconscious Script is composed of four interwoven layers that describe how people do not repeat behaviors because they're irrational or unwilling. They repeat because the reptation induces awareness. And those patterns form long before the conscious mind ever integrates them. The chart, the nervous system, and the lived emotional body all reveal the same thing: we're built from a set of foundational structures that shape how we feel, react, attach, collapse, and evolve.

These patterns begin at the deepest layer — the soul's memory. The chart shows this in the placements that feel heavy, ancient, or too familiar to explain. Pluto carries the souls intention and unresolved emotional attachments; the South Node holds the instinctive behavioral patterns the ego defaults to; Saturn shapes the boundaries of what the psyche can handle at any given stage. These aren't abstract ideas. They are the architecture of your operating system. They decide what feels like danger, what feels like home, and what you unconsciously recreate even while trying to change.

The Layers
1. The Soul-Level Patterns
These are the patterns you inherited from other lifetimes. They are instinctive, somatic, and pre-verbal. Pluto and the South Node describe them clearly: the past-life emotional memory, the unfinished business, the survival instincts that still live in your body. These patterns don't respond to mindset or logic. They only shift when the emotional body recognizes what it's doing in real time. They dissolve through embodiment — through staying present in the moment the instinct wants to take over.

2. The Structural Patterns
This is Saturn's realm: the framework your incarnation is built on. Saturn shows where you lack capacity, where life will repeatedly demand maturity, and where the psyche must grow before anything else can change. These patterns aren't wounds so much as absences. They stabilize through repetition, responsibility, and lived experience. Saturn isn't punishment — it's pacing. It sets the emotional limit of what you can hold, and the lifetime becomes the slow work of expanding that limit.

3. The Psychological Patterns
These come from Mercury and Jupiter — the stories you created to

feel safe when your world didn't make sense. These patterns are learned, reinforced, repeated through interpretation. They shift when meaning shifts. They dissolve when the narrative behind them is replaced with one aligned with truth rather than fear. Unlike soul patterns, these do respond to insight, but insight only works when the deeper layers are already being addressed.

4. The Identity Patterns
These live in the Moon and the nodal axis. They describe the emotional atmosphere you were born into, how the ego formed inside a much older karmic story, and how your life keeps steering you toward the North Node whether you want to go or not. These patterns evolve through relationship, environment, and conscious choice. They soften when you stop reenacting outdated emotional contracts and start choosing choices that feel unfamiliar but true.

How the Script Operates Without Your Awareness
The unconscious script is not subtle. It directs your life with the force of memory, instinct, and unfinished karmic tension. But because it speaks through emotion and your nervous system rather than language, most people never realize they're following it. They think they're choosing freely, reacting honestly, avoiding logically. What they're actually doing is replaying an ancient program the body believes is necessary for survival.

1. It chooses your partners. You don't fall for people randomly. You are magnetized toward the individuals whose energy matches the unresolved material in your system. Your script recognizes them long before your mind does. That's why the "irrational pull" feels cosmic — because it *is* karmic. You are not drawn to the person; you are drawn to the unfinished business. The opposite is true as well: when someone is emotionally steady, available, or aligned with your growth, the script reads it as unfamiliar — and therefore unsafe. Indifference toward healthy connection is not a flaw. It is a signal that your system still confuses stability with danger. Until the script is rewritten at the nervous-system level, attraction will follow the past, not the future.

2. It shapes every emotional reaction. Your reactions are not always about the moment you're in. They are echoes of the moments you never resolved. When someone raises their voice and your body registers threat, when someone withdraws and you feel abandoned, when someone offers help and you feel controlled — the reaction isn't to the person. It is to the emotional memory they activated. The script reenacts wounds that were never metabolized. It makes the present feel like the past, and it makes small moments feel like existential danger. This is why insight alone doesn't shift patterns: your body is reacting from a memory that is older than your awareness.

3. It determines what you avoid. Avoidance is not personality. It is conditioning in disguise. What you avoid — confrontation, intimacy, visibility, stillness, change — is often the exact realm your soul came here to master. The script protects the wound by keeping you far from the experiences that could heal it. Avoidance is the ego's attempt to protect the body from material it believes is too overwhelming. But growth requires contact. Every avoided experience holds the key to a part of you that has not yet been lived.

4. It creates your illusions and disillusionments. Through Neptune's function, the script teaches by revealing what was never real. You build identities, fantasies, hopes, and emotional bonds that feel transcendent — until they dissolve. The collapse isn't punishment. It is clarity. Neptune removes the illusion so the soul can stop living through projection. What falls apart under Neptune is not a loss. It is truth reclaiming the space where fantasy used to live.

5. It pulls you into crisis when evolution is blocked. Crisis is the soul's intervention. It is the moment the script refuses to let you stay where you are. When the ego resists change, life applies pressure: endings, breakdowns, revelations that cannot be ignored. The script will repeat the same storyline — the same crisis in different forms — until you embody a different response. That is how patterns end. That is how evolution begins. The script is not your enemy. It is your unfinished story, asking to be rewritten through consciousness, presence, and the courage to finally feel what you once survived by avoiding.

How the Script Develops in Childhood

Contrary to modern psychological models, childhood does not create your deepest wounds. Childhood only activates the wounds your soul brought in. The South Node is your pre-existing emotional blueprint. Your family mirrors it perfectly. Your childhood environment is not the cause but the catalyst. This is why two siblings raised in the same home have different wounds: each is living their own karmic script. Early childhood: confirms your preexisting fears, reenacts unresolved past-life dynamics, teaches the body its first survival strategies, binds the karmic story to this lifetime, shapes your Moon (emotional instinct), Saturn (conditioning). The ego is built inside the karmic echo. By age 7, the script is fully installed.

Crisis as Script Disruption

Crisis is not the moment your life falls apart. Crisis is the moment your script can no longer sustain the version of you that refuses to evolve. When the soul needs to move you toward your North Node — toward the part of your chart that represents growth, expansion, destiny, and becoming — it uses disruption as a catalyst. The ego never chooses these turning points. The soul does. When the unconscious script has held you in a loop for too long, the psyche begins to destabilize the very structures you built for safety. Relationships dissolve. Jobs collapse. Certainty unravels. The body reacts with panic, shaking, overwhelm, or shutdown. Your identity cracks open, not because you did something wrong, but because the next version of your life cannot grow inside the old one.

Crisis is not punishment — it's **re-routing**.
Saturn initiates crises of structure. It exposes where you've outgrown your foundations. It collapses commitments that no longer reflect who you are. It forces maturation through discomfort, but always toward alignment. When a Saturn crisis arrives, the soul is saying: *Your life must be rebuilt on truth, not habit.*

The Sun – Crisis of Identity

The Sun is activated when the identity you are performing is no longer authentic. This shows up as exhaustion, loss of vitality, depression, or a sense that you are "playing a role" in your own life. The external life may look successful, but internally you feel hollow or invisible. The Sun destabilizes confidence when confidence is no longer rooted in truth.

Sun crises force you to ask: Who am I without approval, achievement, or recognition? This is often triggered through burnout, leadership failure, or situations where your authority is questioned. The ego resists because the Sun is attached to dignity and self-definition. But the soul is asking you to *be*, not perform.

The Moon – Crisis of Emotional Safety

The Moon is activated through crisis when your emotional coping mechanisms are outdated. This is the moment when the ways you soothe yourself no longer work. Anxiety spikes. Old wounds surface. You feel unsafe without knowing why. Relationships that once felt comforting start to feel suffocating or destabilizing. Moon crises are often misdiagnosed as "overreaction," but they are signals that your nervous system has outgrown its early conditioning. The Moon asks: What do you need now, not what once kept you alive? These crises often involve family, home, caretaking roles, or emotional dependency. The body leads here, not logic.

Mercury – Crisis of Narrative
Mercury crisis happens when the story you tell yourself can no longer organize your experience. You may feel mentally scattered, confused, unable to concentrate, or stuck in obsessive thinking loops. Communication breaks down. Misunderstandings multiply. You realize your beliefs no longer match reality. Mercury crises dismantle certainty. They force you to question: What if the way I think about this is the problem? This often appears through information overload, contradictory feedback, or conversations that shatter assumptions. The ego resists because Mercury likes coherence. But the soul wants *accuracy*, not comfort.

Venus – Crisis of Value and Attachment
Venus crisis occurs when your values and relationships are misaligned with your self-worth. This is where love stops feeling nourishing. Where beauty feels empty. Where desire no longer matches reality. Relationships end not because they are "bad," but because they reflect an old version of your worth. Venus crises ask: What do you tolerate because you don't believe you deserve more? These often come through heartbreak, financial instability, or the collapse of aesthetics, identities, or pleasures that once soothed you. The ego clings because Venus wants harmony. The soul demands authenticity.

Mars – Crisis of Will and Direction
Mars crisis occurs when your actions are disconnected from your truth.
You may feel restless, irritable, angry, or blocked. Motivation collapses or explodes destructively. Conflict increases because suppressed desire seeks expression. Mars crises ask: What do you want that you are afraid to claim?
These often involve power struggles, burnout, physical symptoms, or impulsive behavior. The ego fears loss of control. The soul wants *aligned action*, not endless effort.

Jupiter – Crisis of Meaning

Jupiter crisis occurs when the belief system you live by no longer makes sense. Faith collapses. Optimism fades. The future feels vague or empty. What once inspired you now feels inflated or false. This is existential crisis territory. Jupiter asks: What do you believe, and is it actually true? These crises often come through disillusionment with teachers, institutions, ideologies, or long-term goals. The ego resists because Jupiter loves certainty and hope. The soul requires *truth*, even if it's uncomfortable.

Saturn – Crisis of Structure
Saturn initiates crisis when the structures you rely on are no longer sustainable. This is the collapse of careers, timelines, commitments, and identities built on endurance rather than alignment. Life feels heavy. Progress slows. Consequences appear. Saturn asks: What are you building, and why?
These crises are often labeled as "failure," but they are corrections. Saturn strips away what is no longer viable so something more honest can be built. The ego resists because Saturn threatens security. The soul needs integrity.

Uranus – Crisis of Freedom
Uranus initiates crisis when your life has become too predictable, controlled, or restrictive. Sudden changes occur. Shocks. Breakups. Radical decisions. You feel electrified or destabilized. The nervous system spikes. Uranus asks: Where are you living someone else's version of your life? These crises feel abrupt because Uranus operates faster than consciousness. The ego panics because it loses control. The soul is reclaiming autonomy.

Neptune – Crisis of Illusion
Neptune initiates crisis when the fantasy collapses.
Confusion, exhaustion, grief, disillusionment. The thing you believed would save you dissolves. Meaning blurs. Motivation fades. You can no longer pretend. Neptune asks: What are you avoiding feeling? These crises feel like loss, but they are awakenings. Neptune removes false meaning so real meaning can emerge. The ego feels unmoored. The soul is dissolving what is unreal.

Pluto – Crisis of Death and Rebirth
Pluto initiates crisis when a core identity must die. This is non-negotiable. Power dynamics collapse. Control fails. Trauma surfaces.

Obsessions intensify. Something fundamental ends. Pluto asks: What are you clinging to that is already dead? These crises feel extreme because they are. But they are also final. Pluto does not destabilize to adjust. It destabilizes to transform. The ego experiences annihilation. The soul experiences liberation.

The body often interprets all these shifts as danger. Panic attacks, emotional collapses, uncontrollable grief, and somatic unraveling are the nervous system's response to the ego losing its script. But this dismantling is not regression — it is rewiring. In crisis, you are not falling apart. You are being reorganized around a new truth. Crisis is the soul saying: *You are done here. Move.*

The ego hears this as threat. The soul knows it as evolution. Every dismantling is a directional change. Every collapse is a doorway. Every breakdown is the point where the old pattern can no longer continue. Crisis is not the place where you failed; it is the place where the curriculum intensifies. It is the moment the unconscious script stops controlling you and begins revealing itself — giving you the chance to choose differently, to step toward the North Node, and to live from the self you came here to become.

The Script Is Activated by Transit Cycles
For as long as I can remember, my life has been a laboratory for this work. It has been my purpose — sometimes willingly, sometimes painfully — to observe, document, and decode every phase of these unfolding. I've spent decades tracing the mechanics of how a soul evolves through pressure, disruption, and collapse. And not just the stories we tell, but the somatic truth beneath them: the difference between a trauma response and an actual evolved response, sign by sign, planet by planet. Because the script is never random. It is activated by timing.

The unconscious script doesn't move all at once; it opens in layers, each one initiated by a planetary cycle designed to bring you into deeper contact with what you came here to heal. The transits don't force evolution — they reveal where evolution is blocked. They bring the unconscious into the body so you can finally recognize what's been directing you from beneath your awareness.

Saturn: When Saturn moves through key areas of your chart, it initiates a slow, sobering cycle that lasts 2–3 years. These aren't casual growth phases they're milestones of maturity, often marked by fatigue, emotional solitude, or a sense that something once reliable no longer fits. Think of Saturn transits as reality checks from your future self. They tend to arrive every 7 years or so, spotlighting life chapters that need restructuring. Patterns built on avoidance begin to collapse. Superficial careers, draining relationships, or misaligned goals can no longer be sustained.

Saturn doesn't punish — it clarifies. It reveals what lacks endurance and asks, *Is this sustainable? Is this true?* The pressure often comes through loss, delay, or internal frustration — not to destroy, but to refine. There's a karmic undertone too: what you've neglected demands attention, and what you've cultivated with care gains momentum. It's a season that separates what you *want* from what you're truly *ready to hold*. Boundaries become essential, time feels limited, and anything rooted in fantasy is replaced by what can actually endure. Saturn teaches that real freedom is built through responsibility — and anything misaligned is quietly, or loudly, removed.

Uranus: Uranus doesn't ask for permission. It rips the rug out — not to hurt you, but to expose where you've settled for less than truth. These transits can feel like lightning in slow motion: unpredictable, destabilizing, often uncomfortable… but always revealing. They unravel the parts of your life built on autopilot. During a Uranus transit your nervous system becomes the battleground for freedom. Relationships, careers, even identities can fall apart — not randomly, but because your soul needs a different blueprint. One that's actually yours. It's rarely graceful. The changes feel sudden, and often they come before you feel ready. But what looks like chaos is actually precision — Uranus is here to release you from the patterns you didn't know you were trapped in. The masks that used to keep you safe start to itch. The routines that once felt reliable begin to suffocate.

Uranus transits can bring anxiety, rebellion, insomnia, and emotional volatility — not as flaws, but as signals. Something inside you is trying to awaken. Something long buried is ready to be lived. The key isn't control — it's curiosity. These are moments where you learn to surrender to your own evolution. Uranus doesn't destroy just to destroy. It clears space for your real life to begin.

Neptune: A Neptune transit is like walking through fog with a candle. The edges blur. Certainties melt. Things you thought were solid — your goals, your relationships, your identity — start to feel strangely distant, as if they're being washed out by an invisible tide. You might call it confusion. You might call it loss. But what's really happening is surrender. This is the realm of the sacred undoing. Neptune invites you into deeper intimacy with the unseen — the soul behind the structure, the truth beneath the performance. But first, it removes the filters. You'll lose your taste for surface things. You'll crave more meaning, more softness, more truth. And you'll grieve, because the world rarely offers it in the ways you hoped.

Neptune transits (often lingering for years) test your discernment. Illusions become seductive. You might spiritualize what hurts, romanticize what drains you, or numb out with distractions that feel like devotion. Watch your escapism. Watch your fantasies. Not to judge them — but to understand what they're protecting.

Pluto: Pluto doesn't ask politely. It drags you under. A Pluto transit isn't subtle. It's not a gentle growth curve or a nudge toward change — it's a full psychic excavation. Whatever is false, fragile, or borrowed must die. Not to hurt you, but to reveal what's indestructible beneath. These transits (which can last several years) usher in soul-level metamorphosis. You lose jobs, identities, relationships — anything that gave you a false sense of power or security. At first, it feels brutal. Lonely. Like something is being ripped from you. But eventually, you see: nothing real is ever destroyed. Only what you were clinging to.

Pluto transits activate your deepest unconscious patterns. Attachment wounds. Control strategies. Generational pain. It brings it all up — not in whispers, but in sirens. And you can't bypass it with affirmations or spiritual detours. Pluto isn't impressed by masks. It wants your rawness. It wants you undone. It rules death, yes — but also resurrection. The fire burns everything that is not you, but what remains is elemental. Real. The self you rebuild after Pluto has visited you is not the self who entered. It's the version that can't be manipulated, drained, or broken again. Pluto brings power. But only after it teaches humility.

The Nodes: You feel it in the tension between comfort and calling. Between what you know how to do… and what you secretly ache to become. North Node invitations feel terrifying and exhilarating at once — because they require the death of your smaller self. Every major turning point? A Node is involved. Nodal transits, returns (around age 19 and 38), and conjunctions to personal planets act like cosmic plot twists. They yank you back onto your soul's path. The wrong job collapses. The karmic lover arrives. The old pattern finally snaps. You can't fake it anymore. But here's the paradox: you're not supposed to abandon the South Node. You're supposed to integrate it. It holds your innate gifts — your medicine. But those gifts have to be reoriented toward growth, not comfort. You bring the wisdom of the past forward, then step into the unfamiliar future.

How the Script Becomes Conscious

Becoming conscious of your script is not an intellectual event. It isn't something you understand, analyze, or "figure out." The script lives beneath language — in sensation, impulse, overwhelm, attraction, avoidance, collapse, and the emotional residue that lingers long after a moment has passed. Consciousness doesn't come from thinking about these patterns. It comes from feeling them without abandoning yourself. The script becomes conscious the moment you stop interpreting your reactions as personality and begin recognizing them as patterns. Not character flaws. Not fate. Not "just how you are." Patterns. Old ones. Ones that formed long before your adult self had any say in the matter.

And each pattern has a different mechanism. Some are karmic. Some are somatic. Some are psychological. Some are identity-based. Some live in the nervous system; others live in the story you told yourself to make sense of a world that didn't know how to hold you. This is why one method of healing can never be universal. How you work with a pattern depends entirely on its function.

- A Pluto pattern must be met in the body — in tremor, in panic, in grief that feels older than your lifetime.
- A Saturn pattern must be matured — patiently, slowly, through lived responsibility.
- A Neptune pattern must be clarified — through dissolving fantasy and reclaiming discernment.
- A Mercury pattern must be reframed — through new meaning and accurate interpretation.
- A lunar pattern must be re-parented — through safety, tenderness, and emotional repair.

You cannot treat every script the same way because every script is born from a different layer of you. Consciousness begins with recognition. You notice the moment your chest tightens before you speak. You feel the impulse to run when someone gets close. You catch the split-second drop in your stomach when someone raises their voice. At first, it feels like your life is exposing you. Then you realize: this is the pattern revealing itself. This is the exact material you're meant to meet.

The script becomes conscious when you stay with yourself in the moment you would normally collapse, numb, attack, appease, or disappear. Your job is not to change the reaction. Your job is to recognize who in you is reacting: the child, the survivor, the protector, the part of you that believed love had conditions, the part that learned safety through silence. When you stay present with the sensation instead of performing the pattern, the unconscious loses its power. Awareness enters the body. The reaction slows. The nervous system begins to learn something new: I can feel this without reliving the past. I can stay present without being destroyed. I can choose instead of reenact.

This is the moment the script becomes editable. The mechanics of your book exist to guide this exact process — to teach the reader how to identify the function of a pattern, locate its origin, understand its planetary architecture, and work with it through the correct doorway: somatic, emotional, psychological, narrative, or karmic. Consciousness is not the end of the script. It is the beginning of authorship.

The Language You Need
We have so many tools available to us, yet the persistent one that I needed and likely why you're reading this book- is the one that doesn't exist. By the time you reach your 30's you probably have studied every possible self help book written. The language we were always missing was the integrated universal language of the soul. If you're holding this book, chances are you've already tried everything else. You've read psychology. You've analyzed your childhood to the bone. You've memorized attachment styles, trauma loops, and the inner-child scripts. You've taken spiritual courses, listened to intuitive teachers, studied astrology, maybe even pulled your own chart a hundred times hoping something would "click." And still… something didn't add up.

That's usually how the search begins: not with answers, but with the sense that every answer you did find was missing a hidden layer. Maybe you noticed that therapy helped you understand the behavior but not stop repeating it. Astrology gave you insight but didn't explain why certain patterns refused to change no matter how much shadow work you did. Manifestation teachings worked sometimes — but collapsed during the moments you needed them most. You start to wonder if you're the problem. Or whether the universe is punishing you.

The truth — and this is the thing that's so hard to name until you live through it — is that psychology can't touch your soul patterns, and spirituality can't override your nervous system. Astrology describes architecture, but it doesn't teach the language of the unconscious. You needed a system that explained all of it together — the emotional body, the psyche, the chart, the nervous system, the ancestors, the karmic memory, and the lived moment you're standing in. You didn't need more information, you need a language for your life. And most of us don't realize how hungry we were for that language until everything starts repeating.

Maybe it was the same breakup with a different face. Maybe it was the same job ending in the same way, no matter how hard you tried. Maybe you kept attracting the same emotional dynamic — abandonment, betrayal, rejection, chaos, instability — and you couldn't explain why.

On paper, you were intelligent, self-aware, emotionally literate. You could articulate your feelings better than most. You had insight, intuition, and probably a decent sense of spirituality. And yet the pattern didn't care. It kept happening. That's the moment most people find astrology again — not as entertainment, not as personality analysis, but as a map of something deeper, older, and far more precise than psychology ever accounted for. Because the chart doesn't describe your personality, It describes your memory.

Not the memory your conscious mind holds — the memory your soul holds. The memory your body holds. The memory your life keeps circling back to. And once the pattern begins repeating with enough intensity, you realize something quietly devastating: You've been speaking to your unconscious in the wrong language your entire life. You've been trying to negotiate with your pain using logic. You've been trying to soothe your nervous system with insight. You've been trying to heal karmic wounds with affirmations. It's like trying to fix a glitch in the operating system by rearranging the icons on the desktop. You needed a language for the system itself. A language for the part of you that existed before your personality. A language for the part of you that keeps creating the same experience even when you "know better."

Not because you need more information, but because you need recognition — the relief of hearing your inner world described in a way that finally feels accurate. Because once the unconscious is given the correct language, the pattern is no longer running you. You are reading it. And the moment you can read your soul's architecture; your life starts making sense in a way it never has before.

The Limits of Psychology, Spirituality, and Surface Astrology
One of the most frustrating moments on the healing path is when you finally understand why you do what you do — and it still doesn't change anything. You name the pattern. You trace it back to childhood. You articulate the wound perfectly. You even catch yourself in the moment you're repeating it. And then, without fail, you watch the same reaction fire through your body like a reflex you never authorized.

It doesn't matter how self-aware you are. It doesn't matter how many breakthroughs you've had in therapy. Your system acts before your mind has time to negotiate with it. It almost makes you feel broken. You're not. Here's the thing hardly anyone says clearly: Insight is not integration. Knowing is not the same as healing. And understanding the pattern intellectually doesn't change the unconscious contract underneath it.

That's where psychology hits its limit. Therapy can help you name your childhood wound, but it can't show you why the wound repeats across lifetimes or why you keep magnetizing the same archetype in different people. It can help you see your triggers, but it can't explain why those triggers ignite at predictable astrological cycles. And no amount of cognitive reframing can dissolve a karmic imprint encoded in your emotional body. It's not that psychology is wrong. It's just incomplete. And spirituality — at least the modern, polished, Instagram-ready version — often ends up doing the same thing in reverse. You're told to "vibrate higher," "manifest differently," or "align with abundance" without anyone explaining why your nervous system is still wired for survival or why your unconscious rejects what your conscious mind thinks it wants.

You can't mantra your way out of a Pluto wound. You can't visualize your way out of a Saturn contract. You can't "love and light" your way through Uranus detonating your old identity. Spirituality often gives you permission to dream, but not the tools to understand the machinery of the self that keeps pulling you back into the same loop. And then — usually after enough cycles, disappointments, and "Why is this happening again?" moments — you return to astrology with different eyes. Not the pop astrology that talks about confidence because you're a Leo Sun or emotional depth because you're a Scorpio Moon. Not the archetype lists that give you traits like bullet points on a personality exam. You begin to sense that the chart is actually describing something much more profound:

> The Unconscious Structure of Your soul.
> The Blueprint of Your Emotional History.
> The Pattern you Incarnated to Resolve.
> The Evolutionary Cycles of Generations.

Suddenly your Saturn placement doesn't feel like a random struggle — it feels like the karmic lesson encoded into your psyche. Your Pluto sign doesn't feel like a dark coincidence — it feels like the emotional underworld you've been carrying since before this lifetime. Your Nodes describe your most instinctive behaviors and your most uncomfortable growth edges with eerie precision. And once you understand this, the old frustration you felt toward yourself softens. You realize you weren't "failing at healing." You were speaking the wrong language.

You were trying to resolve a soul-level contract with psychological tools designed for the mind. You were trying to soothe a nervous system wound with spiritual metaphors. You were trying to correct a karmic pattern with conscious behavioral changes. No wonder it didn't work. No wonder you felt like you were walking in circles. No wonder everything repeated until you thought you were cursed. Here's the truth that most people never get to hear until their mid-thirties, when life has exhausted all their other options:

> Your soul patterns do not respond to insight. They respond to recognition.
> To being seen by you. To being understood in their native language.

You deserve to understand your internal world through the lens that finally makes sense. Not the lens of pathology. Not the lens of self-blame. Not the lens of spiritual bypassing. But the lens of your soul. The moment you start seeing yourself through that lens, your entire life begins to reorganize around it — gently, quietly, but unmistakably. This is the beginning of that reorganization.

When Life Starts Repeating Itself

There comes a point — usually after you've survived enough heartbreaks, job collapses, karmic relationships, confusing synchronicities, and "Why me?" spirals — when something inside you quietly mutters: "Wait... I've been here before." Not literally. Emotionally. The details change — new lover, new boss, new state, new spiritual teacher — but the emotional signature is identical. You can almost taste the déjà vu in your body. And in that moment, you sense a deeper truth rising: Life is not failing you. Life is repeating itself so you finally see the pattern.

It's humbling, almost eerie, when this realization lands. You start recalling every chapter of your life and noticing the same story playing under the surface like a soundtrack you missed because you were too busy surviving. You remember every relationship that left you feeling unchosen. Every workplace where your brilliance dissolved into burnout. Every friendship where you became the healer instead of the human. Every spiritual journey where you hoped the next insight would "finally fix it." Every moment you collapsed into the same emotion you thought you healed five years ago.

And suddenly, the question shifts from "Why is this happening?" to: "What is this trying to show me?"

That shift alone is revolutionary, because once you ask that question, the unconscious begins to respond. Not in words, but in symbols, sensations, and patterns that keep circling back like a cosmic echo. And this is where astrology stops being entertainment and becomes revelation. Because your chart — the thing you've probably glanced at a thousand times — starts revealing itself as a map of these patterns. Not metaphorically. Literally.

The same archetypes that keep showing up in your life also live in your chart. If you look closely, you'll notice: The wound that keeps repeating has the emotional fingerprint of your Moon or Chiron. The crisis you keep attracting has the intensity of Pluto. The instability you keep blaming yourself for carries the lightning signature of Uranus. The lessons you avoid have Saturn's handwriting all over them. The longing you can't stop chasing whispers through your South Node. The thing you deeply want but feels uncomfortable? That's your North

Node calling.

And here's where people usually break down — not out of despair, but relief: You finally realize you're not defective. You're patterned. And patterned does not mean doomed. Patterned means intelligent. Patterned means purposeful. Patterned means you incarnated with a curriculum. But until someone hands you the language to interpret that curriculum, your life looks like a chaotic mess of coincidences and personal failures. It's not. It's the same archetype moving through different forms, trying to get your attention.

Let me say that again, because it changes everything: A soul pattern does not stop repeating until the unconscious becomes conscious — not intellectually, but emotionally and somatically. And so many people spend decades fighting themselves because they try to solve a soul-level pattern with surface-level logic. They leave the relationship but keep the wound. They switch careers but carry the same insecurity. They relocate to a new state but feel the same emotional atmosphere. They learn astrology but stop at personality traits instead of shadow contracts. They meditate until they're numb but never touch the instinct underneath the trigger.

At some point, you realize that the problem isn't your effort — it's your operating system. You've been using conscious tools to solve unconscious architecture. And unconscious architecture only responds to one thing: Recognition. Noticing. Awareness without self-attack. Truth without trying to fix it. That's when you begin to sense something far more mysterious: the universe has been speaking to you through patterns your whole life. And not just outer patterns, but inner ones — emotional déjà vu, repeating dreams, cycles of collapse and rebirth that sync with your transits whether you believe in them or not.

This is the moment — right here — where people usually feel two things at the same time: A strange comfort. And a terrifying clarity. Comfort, because for the first time, your life makes sense. Clarity, because now you know you can't unsee it. Once you see the pattern, the pattern becomes your teacher. Once you understand the archetype, the archetype becomes your guide. Once you recognize the soul contract, the contract begins to dissolve. And this… this is where we begin.

When Your Tools Stop Working

There's a strange moment that happens somewhere in your mid-thirties — sometimes earlier, sometimes later — when every method you've used to keep your life "together" simply... stops cooperating. It's almost comical, except it's not. It's terrifying. You meditate but feel nothing. You journal but gain nothing. You manifest but nothing arrives. You pray but feel unheard. You script, visualize, affirm — and reality does not move. Not even an inch.
It feels like the universe suddenly unplugged from your frequency. Like you're knocking on a door that used to open easily. Like you're speaking a language no one understands anymore. And for a little while, you think something's wrong with you. Are you depressed? Blocked? Unaligned? Out of faith? Being punished?

It's so easy to spiral into old fear narratives, especially if you spent years relying on these tools to stay afloat. But here's the truth — the one people rarely say out loud because it doesn't fit neatly into a motivational quote: Your tools stopped working because you outgrew the identity they belonged to. Manifestation techniques only work within the identity structure that created them. Therapy tools only work within the ego structure they were designed to manage. Spiritual rituals only work when they match the frequency of the self performing them.

When the identity begins to dissolve — even if you haven't consciously realized it yet — the universe stops reinforcing the version of you that those tools were created for. That's not failure. That's evolution. You know what it feels like? It feels like the universe quietly saying: "Sweetheart, you can't use this to stabilize a self that no longer exists." It's unsettling on a level that's hard to describe unless you've lived through it. Everything you used to rely on now feels strangely hollow, faded, almost like trying to turn the doorknob on a house you moved out of. This is where most people panic. Not because they lack faith — but because their identity is dissolving beneath them.

Identity Dissolution
Feels like emotional flatness, boredom that borders on existential, a loss of desire, a loss of intuition, a silence where your guidance used to be, a strange sense that life has no "instructions" anymore. It's not depression, though it can mimic it. It's the nervous system loosening its grip on your old self. See, as long as you were operating from an identity built on fear, survival, scarcity, perfectionism, validation-seeking, or childhood adaptation, your tools worked for that identity.

They maintained it. They stabilized it. They kept the scaffolding in place.

But the moment the soul decides: "We're not doing that anymore," everything collapses. Not to harm you — but to free you. To force you inward. To remove what can no longer come with you. To make you turn toward a part of yourself you have avoided your entire life. And here's where the language of the soul becomes crucial. Because at this point, your mind will absolutely lie to you. It will insist something is wrong. That you're failing. That you're regressing. Your mind will speak in panic. Your soul will speak in symbols. And the body? The body will speak in sensations you don't yet understand.

This is the juncture where astrology becomes more than a symbolic framework — it becomes a steady hand on your shoulder. Because your chart will show you that the collapse you're experiencing syncs perfectly with transits you didn't choose and cannot control. Your Progressed Moon moves into the 12th house and your desires evaporate. Neptune touches your Sun and your identity dissolves. Pluto aspects your Moon and the emotional body purges old selves. Saturn crosses your Ascendant and your old personality dies. Uranus hits an angle and your life fractures open. None of this is personal. None of it is punishment. None of it is a failure. It's timing.

The timing you agreed to. The timing your soul prepared for. The timing that forces you to stop interpreting symptoms as catastrophe and start seeing them as initiation. Think back — has your life ever actually evolved in the absence of discomfort? Has anything meaningful ever been birthed without some kind of dissolution first? No.

Every psychological breakthrough began with confusion. Every spiritual awakening began with emptiness. Every identity shift began with loss. So when your tools stop working, it is not a sign of regression. It is a sign that you are entering the deeper work — the part no one teaches because it cannot be taught, only lived. This is where your soul begins speaking in a much older, more cryptic language. The kind of language you can't interpret unless someone shows you how. And that's what this book is going to do — give you the language no one gave you when your world began to fall apart. In other words, welcome to the beginning.

3 SOUL PATTERNS

Soul Patterns are the underlying currents shaping your emotional landscape, your relationships, your choices, your resistance, your desires, your fears, your karmic echoes, and the very architecture of how your consciousness experiences life. They are not fated outcomes. They're frameworks. Blueprints. Echoes of where your soul has been and where it's trying to go. You've lived inside these patterns your whole life, even before you knew they existed. You've followed them instinctively — sometimes willingly, often unconsciously. Every major turning point in your life, every heartbreak that shattered you, every job you walked away from, every person who triggered something ancient inside you, every collapse that forced you inward — all of it was shaped by these deeper, older, more intelligent patterns. Not because you chose them. Because they came with you.

They're the emotional fingerprints of your chart. The places where your soul has unresolved business. The places where it carries memory, desire, instinct, and unfinished themes. And once you start recognizing them — once you name them — everything in your life suddenly becomes readable. "Why does this always happen to me?" Because the pattern hasn't been integrated yet. "Why do I attract people like this?" Because your soul is speaking a language you haven't learned to decode. "Why do I keep running from stability?" Because the version of you shaped by fear has not yet met the identity shaped by truth. "Why does healing feel cyclical?" Because evolution is rhythmic, not linear.

The Map Beneath the Map
Your birth chart is a living document. A biography written in symbols.

But beneath the symbols lies the deeper story — the unconscious motivations that govern your inner life long before a transit ever activates them. Most people come to astrology looking for prediction. But the truth is, prediction is the least interesting part. The power of astrology is that it reveals why you are the way you are. Why your nervous system responds the way it does. Why you're drawn to certain people. Why you can't tolerate certain environments. Why you repeat certain emotional loops. Why certain themes follow you across decades, relationships, and entire chapters of life.

Soul patterns live in:
– your lunar Nodes (the karmic compass)
– your Pluto placement (the souls evolutionary intent)
– your Saturn placement (the karmic lesson)
– your Chiron (the wound and gift)
– your Moon (the ego identity)
– your Mercury (the perception and interpretative mind)
– your Venus (the feeling and relational blueprint)
– your progressed Moon cycles (the identity shifts)
– your Jupiter conjunct sun cycles (Identity Evolution)

And here's what most people don't realize: Your soul patterns activate before you're conscious enough to interpret them. This is why your early life shapes so much of your adulthood. Not because childhood defines you — but because it awakens the patterns you incarnated to work with. Think of it like this: Your soul brings the blueprint. Your childhood provides the stage. Your adulthood becomes the translation. You're not here to fix your past. You're here to understand the pattern that shaped it.

The nature and function of soul patterns are not random. They're intelligent, cosmic, archetypal. And if you're anything like me, you probably learned this the hard way—through painful cycles that refused to budge no matter how many psychological theories you dissected or how deep you wandered into your own shadow.

The Four Archetypal Patterns
One of the most confusing parts of healing is that some patterns soften the moment you understand them, while others refuse to budge no matter how much insight you gain. Some respond to reframing. Others only shift when the body learns safety. Others don't respond to any "work" at all and instead unfold through time, loss, and initiation. This is not because you are doing something wrong. It is

because not all patterns originate from the same layer of consciousness. Your psyche is not a single system. It is layered. And each layer speaks a different language. Through years of observation, lived experience, and astrological study, I've found that repeating patterns fall into four primary categories. Each one forms differently, repeats differently, and requires a completely different method of integration. When people struggle endlessly to change a pattern, it's usually because they are applying the wrong tool to the wrong category. Before you try to heal anything, you must first identify *what kind of pattern you are dealing with*.

These patterns fall into four distinct archetypes—each shaped by a different layer of your consciousness. Once you understand which one you're dealing with, the entire healing process becomes clearer. Not easier, but finally coherent.

BELIEF PATTERNS
Interpretive Structures
Belief patterns live in the mind. They form through interpretation, not trauma alone. These are the conclusions you drew when life didn't make sense and you needed a framework to survive inside it. They answer questions like: *What does this mean? How does the world work? What does this say about me?* These patterns are governed by Mercury and Jupiter, the planets that shape perception, meaning, and worldview. Belief patterns repeat through thought loops, assumptions, and self-talk. They often sound logical, even when they are painful. Because they live at the level of meaning, belief patterns *can* change through insight—but only when the insight reaches the original interpretation that created them. Trying to somatically heal a belief pattern without updating its meaning often leads to frustration and self-blame.

REJECTED ARCHETYPAL PATTERNS
Suppressed Instincts
Rejected archetypal patterns do not form through thinking. They form through *inhibition*. These are the parts of you that became unsafe to express in your early environment and were quietly shut down so you could belong, attach, or survive. These patterns live in the sign polarities of the chart. They show up through projection, irritation, attraction, and repeated relational mirrors. What you reject internally tends to confront you externally. What you suppress seeks expression through others. These patterns do not change through insight alone, because they are not beliefs. They are instinctual

suppressions. They heal through conscious embodiment and reclamation, not analysis. You don't "fix" these patterns—you reintegrate them.

SOMATIC & KARMIC PATTERNS
Nervous-System Memory

Somatic and karmic patterns live in the body, not the mind. They form before language, often before conscious memory, and sometimes before this lifetime entirely. These patterns are carried through the nervous system, ancestral inheritance, and karmic memory. Governed by Pluto, Chiron, and the South Node, these patterns activate instantly. They show up as reflexes, panic, urgency, collapse, or emotional intensity that feels disproportionate to the present moment. You may understand them perfectly and still feel powerless to stop the reaction. These patterns do not respond to insight, reframing, or positive thinking. They change through presence, regulation, and staying with the body during activation. Trying to "think your way out" of a somatic pattern often makes it worse, not better.

EVOLUTIONARY TIMING PATTERNS
Life-Stage Initiations

Evolutionary timing patterns are not wounds at all. They are initiations. These patterns emerge when an identity has expired and the next version of you is forming. They are governed by Saturn, Uranus, Neptune, and Pluto cycles.

These patterns don't repeat because something is unresolved—they repeat because a chapter is closing. They show up as tools no longer working, identities dissolving, external life rearranging, and a sense that something is ending even before you can name what comes next. These patterns do not heal through effort. They unfold through time, surrender, and participation. Trying to "fix" an evolutionary timing pattern often increases suffering, because the task is not correction—it is transition.

Why Misidentification Creates Suffering

Most people suffer not because their patterns are too complex, but because they misidentify them. They try to calm the body when the issue is meaning. They try to analyze instincts that need embodiment. They try to heal what is actually an initiation. When you apply the wrong method to a pattern, you don't just fail to resolve it—you often deepen shame, believing you are broken, resistant, or incapable of change. The moment you correctly identify *which layer a pattern comes from*, the struggle softens. You stop fighting yourself. You stop forcing outcomes. You begin working *with* your psyche instead of against it. This chapter exists so you can learn to sort before you solve. Everything that follows builds on this foundation.

BELIEF PATTERNS
What Belief Patterns Are
Belief patterns are **meaning structures**. They are not emotions in themselves, and they are not wounds in the way most people understand trauma. They are the conclusions the psyche formed when it needed coherence in moments that felt confusing, overwhelming, inconsistent, or unsafe. When a child does not yet have power, language, or context, the psyche stabilizes itself through interpretation. It asks, often unconsciously: *What does this mean? How does the world work? What do I need to believe to stay safe inside this experience?* The answers to those questions become belief patterns.

These beliefs are not chosen deliberately. They are adaptive. They allow the mind to organize reality when reality feels unpredictable. In that sense, belief patterns are intelligent. They preserve continuity. They give the psyche something solid to stand on when external conditions cannot be trusted. Because belief patterns originate as interpretations, not injuries, they do not begin as emotional wounds. Emotion comes later. Anxiety, shame, fear, or self-attack are downstream effects. The belief comes first. The feeling follows.

For example, the psyche does not feel anxious and then decide, *"I am not smart enough."* It decides, *"I am not smart enough,"* and then anxiety arises whenever a situation threatens to confirm that conclusion. The emotion is responding to meaning, not creating it. This is why belief patterns often feel logical, convincing, and difficult to challenge. They were formed to explain reality, not distort it. They only become harmful when the interpretation outlives the context it was created in. What once protected you begins to limit you. Understanding this distinction matters. When you treat a belief pattern as an emotional wound, you may try to soothe feelings without ever touching the conclusion that generates them. But when you recognize a belief pattern as an interpretive structure, you gain access to the layer where real change is possible. You stop trying to calm the emotion and begin examining the meaning that keeps producing it.

Belief patterns do not ask to be released through catharsis. They ask to be **updated**.

How Belief Patterns Develop
Belief patterns begin in childhood, not because something is inherently wrong with the child, but because the psyche must adapt before it has language, power, or context. When a child encounters confusion, pressure, inconsistency, or misunderstanding, the mind does what it is designed to do: it tries to make sense of what is happening. This is where belief formation begins.

Mercury's Role: How Meaning Is Formed
Mercury governs how we learn, think, communicate, and perceive reality. It describes the way the mind gathers information and organizes experience. In early life, Mercury is not abstract or analytical. It is immediate, literal, and survival-oriented. When a child's natural way of thinking is supported, reflected, and given time, Mercury develops confidence and flexibility. But when that way of thinking is rushed, corrected, ignored, misunderstood, or compared, the psyche must adapt quickly.

The child does not question the environment. The child questions themselves. This is the critical moment where belief patterns begin to form.
The psyche draws conclusions such as:
- "I think wrong."
- "I don't learn like others."
- "My questions are a problem."
- "I need to be faster, quieter, clearer to be acceptable."

These are not emotional wounds yet. They are **interpretive adjustments**. The mind is learning how to survive inside the conditions it is given. Mercury's job is not to protect truth; it is to create coherence. And coherence, in childhood, often comes at the expense of self-trust. At this stage, the belief is still narrow. It is about *how the mind works*. It has not yet become a statement about worth. That comes next.

Jupiter's Role: Why Meaning Becomes Law
Jupiter takes Mercury's conclusions and expands them into a worldview. While Mercury asks, *"How does this work?"* Jupiter asks, *"What does this mean about me, life, and my place in the world?"* This is where belief patterns solidify.

What began as a situational conclusion becomes a global rule:
- "I don't learn like others" becomes "I'm not smart enough."

- "I need to be careful when I speak" becomes "If I'm wrong, I disappoint people."
- "I get corrected a lot" becomes "Mistakes are dangerous."

Jupiter gives the belief weight, morality, and consequence. It links cognition to belonging. It turns interpretation into identity. This is why belief patterns stop feeling neutral and start feeling existential. A mistake is no longer just a mistake. It becomes evidence. It becomes a verdict. This is why belief patterns carry so much emotional charge later in life. The fear is not about the moment itself. It is about what the moment *means*. Jupiter has taught the psyche that failure equals loss, disappointment, or exclusion. The body responds accordingly. Understanding this progression matters. Mercury forms the belief to survive confusion. Jupiter makes that belief feel absolute. Together, they create patterns that feel like truth, even when they are no longer accurate.

Belief patterns do not persist because you are unaware of them. They persist because they once worked — and were never updated. In the sections that follow, you'll learn how to identify belief patterns in your own life and, just as importantly, how to tell when a pattern does *not* belong to this category at all.

How to Identify a Belief Pattern in Your Life
Belief patterns usually show up as:
- anxiety tied to performance, evaluation, or being seen
- mental spirals
- self-talk after failure
- fear of misunderstanding
- pressure to be "right" or "acceptable"

Diagnostic questions for the reader:
- Does this pattern live primarily in my thoughts?
- Does it activate through interpretation rather than sensation?
- Does insight reduce it once I hit the *right meaning*?

If yes → belief pattern.

What Actually Transmutes Belief Patterns
Meaning repair, Reframing, Updating the original interpretation, Separating context from identity What does NOT work: Somatic discharge alone, Forcing confidence, Spiritual bypass

REJECTED ARCHETYPAL PATTERNS

Rejected archetypal patterns form when being a certain way becomes unsafe. Not unsafe to think about. Unsafe to embody. Unsafe to express, initiate, feel, want, shine, resist, or take up space. These patterns do not arise from misunderstanding or misinterpretation. They arise from inhibition. From moments when the body learned, often very early, that expressing a particular instinct threatened connection, stability, or belonging. When faced with that choice, the psyche does not debate. It adapts.

> The child does not decide, "This trait is wrong."
> The child decides, "I cannot be this and still belong."

That decision happens beneath language. It is somatic, relational, and immediate. The instinct is not questioned or reframed. It is simply turned down, redirected, or shut off. Over time, what was once natural becomes unfamiliar. What was once alive becomes distant. The self reorganizes around what feels allowed. Rejected archetypal patterns answer a different question than belief patterns. They are not asking, "What does this mean?" They are asking: "Who am I allowed to be and still belong?"

Because these patterns are about embodiment rather than interpretation, they do not live in thought. They live in the body, in impulse, in hesitation, in the split-second decision to hold back, soften, shrink, or disappear. They shape personality not through belief, but through absence. What is rejected internally does not vanish. It moves outward. The disowned archetype often reappears through projection, irritation, fascination, or repeated relational dynamics. The psyche keeps encountering the trait externally because it has not yet been reclaimed internally.

This is why rejected archetypal patterns cannot be healed through insight alone. Understanding why you suppressed a part of yourself does not automatically make it safe to express. These patterns heal through integration, not explanation. Through gradually allowing the body to experience what it once learned to avoid. Rejected archetypal patterns are not flaws. They are survival adaptations. They formed to protect belonging.
They persist until the psyche learns that safety no longer requires self-erasure.

How Rejected Archetypal Patterns Develop

Rejected archetypal patterns develop through **relational**

conditioning, not interpretation. They form in moments when a child learns, through direct or indirect feedback, that expressing a particular instinct threatens connection, stability, or safety. This process is not conscious. It does not involve reasoning, meaning-making, or belief formation. It happens at the level of the body and the relational field. The child does not ask, *"Is this true?"* The child asks, *"Will this cost me love?"* When the answer is yes, the instinct is suppressed.

The Moment of Inhibition

Every archetypal instinct begins as something natural and unfiltered. A child moves toward what feels alive: curiosity, assertion, play, intensity, emotion, visibility, autonomy. When that movement is met with discomfort, withdrawal, punishment, ridicule, overwhelm, or inconsistency, the nervous system receives a clear message. Not: *"This is wrong."* But: *"This is not safe here."* At that moment, the psyche makes an adaptive choice. Expression is traded for attachment. Authenticity is exchanged for belonging. The instinct does not disappear, but it is no longer trusted. This is how archetypal rejection begins.

Why the Body, Not the Mind, Stores This Pattern

Rejected archetypal patterns are not stored as thoughts or narratives. They are stored as **inhibition responses**. The body remembers the moment it learned to pause, pull back, soften, or shut down. This is why these patterns feel automatic and difficult to articulate. There is often no clear memory attached to them, only a felt sense of hesitation or discomfort when a certain quality tries to emerge. The body intervenes before the mind has time to explain.

You may notice:
- a sudden urge to tone yourself down
- a reflex to defer, minimize, or withdraw
- discomfort with visibility or assertion
- a feeling of "this isn't me," even when it is

The archetype was not rejected because it was wrong. It was rejected because it disrupted the emotional environment.

How Suppression Turns Into Pattern

Over time, repeated inhibition teaches the psyche that certain qualities must remain dormant. The personality reorganizes around what feels allowed. Traits that once felt natural begin to feel foreign or threatening. The child grows into an adult who no longer recognizes the disowned instinct as part of themselves. This creates an internal imbalance. What is suppressed internally does not vanish. It seeks expression elsewhere. The psyche begins encountering the rejected archetype externally, often in exaggerated or distorted forms. These encounters show up as irritation, judgment, fascination, or recurring relational dynamics. The world appears to be "full of" the very traits the person cannot access in themselves. This is not coincidence. It is compensation.

Why Insight Alone Cannot Resolve These Patterns
Because rejected archetypal patterns did not form through belief, they do not dissolve through understanding. You can know exactly why you learned to suppress a part of yourself and still feel unable to express it safely. These patterns are not asking to be analyzed. They are asking to be *reintroduced*. Integration happens when the body is gradually shown that expressing the suppressed instinct no longer results in loss. Safety must be experienced, not explained. The nervous system has to learn, through lived moments, that embodiment is now possible. Rejected archetypal patterns persist not because you are resistant to change, but because your system is loyal to the conditions it learned in. Healing does not require force. It requires permission, pacing, and re-embodiment. These patterns developed to preserve belonging. They release when the psyche learns that belonging no longer requires self-abandonment.

How to Identify Rejected Archetypal Patterns in Your Life
Rejected archetypal patterns are rarely recognized through thought. They are recognized through **reaction**. These patterns announce themselves not by what you say you want, but by what consistently disturbs, irritates, intimidates, or fascinates you in others. To identify a rejected archetypal pattern, you do not start by looking at your chart. You start by observing your emotional and bodily responses in everyday life.

Notice Who Triggers You by Simply Being Themselves
One of the clearest indicators of a rejected archetype is disproportionate reaction. Not conflict. Not disagreement. But a strong internal response to someone who is not doing anything *to* you. You may notice:
- irritation toward people who take up space easily
- discomfort around those who speak freely or dominate conversation
- resentment toward people who express need, emotion, or desire openly

- judgment of those who seem dramatic, chaotic, passive, intense, confident, or carefree

Ask yourself:
- What quality in this person feels *too much*?
- What part of them feels threatening, embarrassing, or unacceptable?
- Do I feel the urge to shrink, correct, withdraw, or judge?

Often, the quality that disturbs you most is the one you learned not to embody.

Pay Attention to What Feels "Not Like Me"
Rejected archetypal patterns often hide behind identity statements. You may hear yourself say things like:
- "I'm just not that kind of person."
- "I don't do things like that."
- "That's not how I operate."

These statements feel factual, but they often point to early suppression rather than natural absence. The key question is not whether you express a trait now, but whether expressing it ever felt unsafe.

Ask:
- Did this quality feel natural to me at some point?
- Was there a time I learned to tone it down, hide it, or redirect it?
- Do I feel tension or embarrassment imagining myself expressing it?

If imagining embodiment creates discomfort rather than neutrality, you're likely touching a rejected archetype.

Observe Repeating Relational Dynamics
Rejected archetypal patterns often show up through recurring roles in relationships. You may consistently find yourself:
- with partners who embody what you suppress
- overshadowed by louder or more dominant personalities
- attracted to, then resentful of, people who live freely
- placed in roles of support rather than expression

The pattern is not the person. The pattern is the *dynamic*. If you keep encountering the same energetic role in different bodies, you are likely interacting with a disowned instinct seeking integration.

Notice Where You Feel Inhibited Without Clear Reason
Unlike belief patterns, rejected archetypal patterns do not come with a story. They come with hesitation. A pause. A subtle internal "no" that arrives without explanation.

You may notice:
- wanting to speak but stopping yourself
- feeling drawn to act but holding back
- downplaying your presence, desire, or emotion
- softening yourself automatically in certain environments

Ask:
- What am I preventing myself from doing right now?
- What part of me is being managed or contained?
- What feels safer to suppress than express?

The answer often points directly to the rejected archetype.

Why Astrology Comes After Recognition
Only after you recognize the pattern experientially does astrology become useful. The chart does not tell you what you rejected. Your life already has. Astrology simply helps you name the archetypal language of that suppression and understand how integration wants to happen. When you match your lived reactions with sign polarities in the chart, clarity deepens. But the chart should confirm your experience, not override it. A rejected archetypal pattern is not subtle once you know how to look. It shows up in your reactions, your relationships, and your repeated discomfort with particular qualities of being. What you resist externally often reveals what you abandoned internally. And what you abandoned did not leave because it was wrong. It left because it was not safe to stay.

How to Work With Archetypal Qualities
You do not need me to list every archetypal quality for every sign. These qualities are everywhere. Any basic astrology source will show you the core expressions of each sign.

What matters is **how you respond to those qualities**, not memorizing them.
Your task is simple:
1. Look up the core qualities of a sign

2. Observe how you *react* to those qualities in real life
3. Notice where your reaction is distorted, emotional, or charged

That reaction tells you far more than the chart ever could on its own.

The Rule of Rejected Archetypes
When you consistently observe **distorted or exaggerated expressions** of an archetype in others, it often points to a part of yourself that was once unsafe to embody. This does not mean the archetype itself is "bad."
It means your relationship to it is incomplete.

EXAMPLE: The Archetypal Vow
Rejected archetypal patterns almost always begin with a **vow**. Not a conscious promise, but an internal decision made early in life when the psyche is trying to restore safety. The child observes instability, chaos, or inconsistency, and decides—often silently—*I will not be that*.

The Original Environment
Imagine a child who grows up with a parent who is emotionally unstable. The parent is unpredictable, impulsive, self-focused, or unreliable. Their moods dominate the environment. Safety feels inconsistent. The child never knows what version of the parent they'll encounter. Nothing needs to be explicitly said. The nervous system is already learning.

The Vow
At some point, the child makes an internal decision:
- *I will be stable.*
- *I will not be selfish.*
- *I will not be emotional or chaotic.*
- *I will be responsible.*
- *I will hold everything together.*

This vow does not come from virtue. It comes from fear. It is an attempt to create order where none existed.

Over-Identification as Survival
From this vow, certain archetypal qualities become overdeveloped:
- **Taurus**: stability, endurance, staying, holding, grounding
- **Capricorn**: responsibility, self-control, emotional restraint, reliability
- **Libra**: keeping the peace, being fair, not upsetting others

These qualities are not unhealthy in themselves. They become distorted because they are **used defensively**. The child learns: stability equals safety, self-denial equals belonging, control equals love. So they become: overly patient, overly responsible, emotionally contained, dependable to a fault, the one who never needs anything. This is not integration. It is **over-identification**.

What Gets Repressed
At the same time, other archetypal qualities become unsafe to embody: emotional volatility, desire, spontaneity, intensity, self-focus, expression of need. These qualities are unconsciously associated with danger because they resemble the parent's instability. So the psyche pushes them away.

The message becomes: *If I express too much, I become the problem.* So the instinct to feel deeply, want freely, or take up space is suppressed.

How the Pattern Shows Up Later
As an adult, this person may: pride themselves on being "low maintenance", stay too long in unhealthy situations, struggle to receive care, feel irritated by emotionally expressive or needy people, feel secretly resentful while appearing calm and composed. They may repeatedly encounter others who embody what they rejected: emotionally intense partners, unpredictable bosses, expressive or self-focused personalities. The pattern isn't coincidence. It's polarity.

The Archetypal Truth
The vow that once created safety now creates imbalance. Stability without emotional truth becomes stagnation. Responsibility without feeling becomes self-abandonment. Peacekeeping without self-expression becomes resentment. Integration does not mean becoming unstable or selfish. It means allowing **range**.

Learning that:
- stability can coexist with emotion
- responsibility does not require self-erasure
- expressing need does not recreate the past

SOMATIC & KARMIC PATTERNS
Somatic and karmic patterns live in the **body**, not the mind. They do not originate in thought, belief, or interpretation. They predate language, story, and conscious memory. These patterns are encoded directly into the nervous system and carried forward as sensation,

reflex, and emotional intensity. Where belief patterns ask *"What does this mean?"* Somatic and karmic patterns ask a different question entirely: "What must be metabolized, not explained?"

These patterns form when an experience overwhelms the system's capacity to process it in real time. The body does not analyze what is happening. It records it. The memory is stored as tension, urgency, collapse, vigilance, or shutdown. Over time, the original event may be forgotten, but the body continues to respond as if it is still occurring. This is why somatic patterns often feel confusing or frustrating. You may understand them intellectually. You may even see them coming. And yet, when they activate, the reaction happens anyway. The body moves first. The mind arrives later.

Somatic and karmic patterns are not irrational. They are **protective reflexes**. They exist to preserve survival, continuity, and coherence at moments when choice was not available. In many cases, they are inherited through lineage or carried across lifetimes, encoded as instinct rather than narrative. Because these patterns do not live in language, they do not resolve through insight alone. No amount of understanding can convince the nervous system that it is safe. Safety must be *experienced*. The body must learn, through presence and regulation, that the threat has passed. These patterns persist not because you are resistant to change, but because the body is loyal to what once kept you alive. Somatic and karmic patterns do not ask to be fixed. They ask to be **met**.

They soften when the body is allowed to complete what was once interrupted: sensation, feeling, response, or release. Integration happens through containment, pacing, and staying present with the experience as it unfolds, rather than trying to override it. When you recognize a pattern as somatic or karmic, the work changes immediately. You stop demanding explanation from the mind and begin offering safety to the body. And in that shift, something essential relaxes.

How Somatic & Karmic Patterns Develop

Somatic and karmic patterns develop when experience overwhelms the system's capacity to process it in real time. Unlike belief or archetypal patterns, these do not form through interpretation or inhibition. They form through **direct imprint**. When the nervous system does not have the resources to complete an experience—because it is too intense, too sudden, too confusing, or too unsafe—the body records the moment instead of resolving it. The memory is stored as sensation, reflex, and survival response. These patterns develop through four primary pathways.

From Early Overwhelm
In early life, the nervous system is still forming its capacity to regulate stimulation. Experiences that exceed that capacity—chronic stress, emotional unpredictability, lack of attunement, sudden loss, or sustained fear—are not processed cognitively. They are absorbed somatically. The body learns: to brace, to shut down, to stay hypervigilant, to collapse inward. The event itself may not be remembered, but the **response becomes automatic**. The nervous system repeats what it learned because it once worked.

From Ancestral Inheritance
Not all somatic patterns originate in personal experience. Some are inherited through lineage. The nervous system carries more than individual memory; it carries the unresolved survival strategies of those who came before. Chronic stress, displacement, violence, loss, or suppression experienced across generations can be encoded as baseline tension, vigilance, or fear without a personal story attached. The body responds as if danger is imminent, even when the environment is safe. This is not imagination. It is biological memory.

From Karmic Memory
Some patterns cannot be traced to early childhood or family history alone. They feel older, deeper, and strangely familiar. These patterns arise from karmic memory—the residue of experiences carried across lifetimes that were never fully integrated. Karmic patterns often activate around themes of power, loss, abandonment, betrayal, or survival. They surface in moments that feel disproportionate to the present, as if something ancient has been stirred. The emotional intensity does not match the situation because the situation is not the source. The body remembers what the mind cannot.

From Survival Reflexes
At the core of all somatic patterns is the survival reflex. Fight, flight, freeze, collapse, or appeasement are not choices; they are automatic responses designed to preserve life when choice is not available. When these reflexes are activated repeatedly or never allowed to complete, they become patterns. The nervous system continues to

respond to present situations as if they carry the same threat as the original event. This is why you may: react before you can think, feel urgency where none exists, shut down despite conscious desire, say "I don't know why I did that" The body is not malfunctioning. It is remembering.

Why Insight Is Not Enough
Somatic and karmic patterns do not respond to understanding because they were never formed through understanding. Insight may bring awareness, but it does not rewire the nervous system. These patterns respond to **presence during activation**. Change happens in the moment the body expects danger and instead receives safety. When you stay present, regulate, and do not act out the reflex, the nervous system learns something new. Over time, the imprint softens. The reflex loosens. Choice returns. You cannot explain a somatic pattern away. You can only **meet it where it lives**. When these patterns are approached correctly, the work becomes less forceful and more respectful. You stop trying to override the body and begin listening to it. And in that relationship, integration becomes possible.

How to Identify Somatic & Karmic Patterns in Your Life
Somatic and karmic patterns are identified not by what you think, but by **how your body reacts**. These patterns announce themselves through sensation, urgency, and reflex rather than story or explanation. Often, the mind is left trying to catch up to something the body has already decided. To recognize a somatic or karmic pattern, you must learn to listen below thought.

The Reaction Happens Before You Can Think
One of the clearest signs of a somatic or karmic pattern is speed. The reaction arrives instantly, without deliberation or conscious choice. There is little to no internal dialogue beforehand. You may notice: a sudden surge of panic or urgency, tightness in the chest, throat, or stomach, an impulse to run, shut down, appease, or control, emotional intensity that feels immediate and absolute. By the time you realize what's happening, the body is already activated. Ask yourself: Did my body react before I had time to interpret the situation? Did my reaction feel automatic rather than chosen? If yes, you are likely dealing with a somatic or karmic pattern.

The Emotional Intensity Feels Disproportionate
Somatic and karmic patterns often feel "too big" for the moment at hand. The emotional response does not match the present situation,

even though it feels completely real. You may think: "I know this isn't logical, but I can't stop it." "This feels like life or death, even though it isn't." "I've felt this exact panic before, but I don't know why." This disproportion is a key marker. It suggests that the body is responding to **memory**, not the present moment.

The Same Sensation Repeats Across Different Situations
Somatic and karmic patterns often repeat as **felt states**, not identical events. The details change, but the bodily experience is unmistakably the same.
You may notice: the same knot in your stomach in different relationships, the same freeze response in unrelated environments, the same urgency appearing with different people. If the body sensation feels familiar across time and context, you are likely touching a somatic or karmic imprint.

The Body Wants Action, Not Explanation
These patterns often come with a strong impulse to *do something* immediately: escape, fix, control, collapse, appease. The urge is not to understand — it is to **survive**. If the primary experience is compulsion rather than curiosity, the pattern is somatic.

Astrological Clues That Support Identification
Astrology does not diagnose somatic patterns, but it can confirm them.
You may notice: strong Pluto, Chiron, or South Node themes, intense reactions during Pluto, Saturn, or nodal transits, repeated crises that force bodily awareness, patterns tied to survival, power, abandonment, or loss. These indicators support what your body already knows. They do not replace it.

How Somatic & Karmic Patterns Are Integrated
Somatic and karmic patterns are not integrated by eliminating triggers. In fact, even after years of awareness and regulation work, you may still find yourself repeatedly entering situations that activate your nervous system. This does not mean you have failed. It means the work has moved to a deeper layer. At this stage, integration becomes less about calming the reaction and more about listening to what the reaction is trying to protect. Sometimes the nervous system is not reacting because something is unresolved. It is reacting because something true is being avoided. There are moments when the body is not asking to be healed so you can stay in a situation. It is asking to be listened to so you can **leave one**. Many people

unconsciously believe that healing means becoming regulated enough to tolerate dynamics that are misaligned. That is not integration. That is endurance. Somatic wisdom is not about numbing reactivity. It is about restoring trust in the body's intelligence. Integration begins when you stop trying to override the signal and instead ask, *what is my nervous system actually responding to?* Sometimes the answer is old fear. Sometimes it is a present truth you have been repressing in the name of growth, loyalty, or healing. Before interpretation, however, the body must feel safe enough to speak.

What To Do When the Impulse Hits
The Actual Method Your System Responds To. When the impulse rises — the panic, the urgency, the compulsion — you don't analyze it. You don't argue with it. You don't tell yourself you're overreacting.

Your first task is to interrupt the automatic pathway with presence, not logic.

1. **Go to the breath immediately**. Not slow breathing — anchoring breathing. A steady inhale with a slightly longer exhale. This signals to the vagus nerve: "We are not in danger. You can stand down."

2. **Put your hand on your heart or body**. This creates co-regulation inside the self — a repair that never happened in childhood. Your body recognizes the gesture before it recognizes the words.

3. **Acknowledge the fear without shaming it**. Say, internally or out loud: "I feel the panic." "I know you're scared." "You're reacting to something old." Recognition deactivates the survival loop faster than reasoning.

4. **Speak to the younger self who originally learned the pattern**. This is crucial. The somatic memory belongs to them, not the adult you. Tell them calmly: "This is the past. You are safe now. I'm here." This creates a neurological dissonance — the body expects danger, but receives reassurance. That mismatch is how rewiring happens.

5. **Wait for the urgency to fade**. Do nothing else. Don't fix the situation. Don't follow the urge. Don't respond to the trigger. A

somatic pattern dissolves when you can feel the impulse fully without acting it out.

The body learns through experience: "I can feel this and not collapse."
"I can feel this and not run." "I can feel this and still be safe."

Every repetition weakens the neural pathway. Every moment of non-reactivity becomes a new imprint. Somatic healing isn't cognitive — it's biological. It's the slow unwinding of a system that once believed survival depended on that reaction.

When the Impulse Is Not the Past, but Suppressed Anger
Not every surge in the body is a trauma response. Not every impulse needs to be soothed. Sometimes the nervous system is not remembering the past — it is reacting accurately to the present. Suppressed anger often feels similar to anxiety or panic in the body, which is why it is frequently misidentified and prematurely regulated. The difference is subtle but essential. Fear-based somatic patterns are protective. Anger-based patterns are **boundary signals**. When anger has been chronically suppressed, it does not arrive cleanly. It shows up as urgency, agitation, pressure, restlessness, or the impulse to escape. The body mobilizes energy, but the mind tries to calm it instead of listening. This is where many people mistakenly pathologize a healthy signal.

When the Impulse Is Not the Past, but Suppressed Anger
Not every surge in the body is a trauma response. Not every impulse needs to be soothed, reframed, or regulated away. Sometimes the nervous system is not remembering the past — it is **responding accurately to the present**. For years, I believed my repeated urge to leave, to escape, to create distance meant I was avoidant, unhealed, or spiritually bypassing something I was supposed to "work through." I told myself that if I could just stay, regulate better, soften more, understand deeper, the impulse would stop. It didn't.

Because the impulse was not fear. It was **suppressed anger**. Suppressed anger often feels identical to anxiety or panic in the body, which is why it is so easily misidentified. The heart races. The chest tightens. The system mobilizes. There is urgency, agitation, pressure, restlessness, and a powerful need to *get out*. The body feels intolerant of containment. When this happens, the mind is trained to say: *Calm down. You're overreacting. This is your past. Regulate and stay.* But this is where discernment matters. Fear-based somatic responses are **protective**. They arise when the body anticipates danger and are oriented toward safety. When fear is present, slowing the body, grounding, and reassurance bring relief. Once safety is restored, the impulse subsides.

Anger-based somatic responses are **boundary signals**. They arise when something is being violated, overridden, or ignored in real time. When anger is present, calming the body does not resolve the impulse — it only contains it temporarily. The signal returns, often stronger, because the truth beneath it has not been acknowledged. Here is how to tell the difference.

Fear softens when you feel understood. Anger stands taller when you tell the truth. Fear collapses into relief. Anger consolidates into clarity. Fear asks, *"Am I safe?"* Anger asks, *"Why am I still here?"* When the impulse is fear-based, the body wants comfort. When the impulse is anger-based, the body wants **change**. Suppressed anger rarely announces itself as anger. Especially in people who learned early that anger was unsafe, disruptive, or unacceptable. Instead, it disguises itself as anxiety, exhaustion, overwhelm, or the compulsive need to leave. The nervous system mobilizes energy to create space, but the mind interprets that energy as dysregulation rather than information.

This is why so many people are taught to stay in dynamics that are harmful under the belief that leaving means they are unhealed. But sometimes the impulse to leave is not avoidance. It is memory — not of the past, but of **what happens when you stay too long**. The body remembers the cost of staying in systems where: your boundaries are negotiated instead of respected, your emotions are explained away, your anger is reframed as pathology, your truth requires permission.

The impulse to escape in these moments is not a failure of regulation. It is the nervous system saying: *I recognize this pattern, and I will not survive it again.* When anger has been chronically suppressed, it will escalate if ignored. First it whispers as discomfort. Then it pushes as restlessness. Then it demands space as urgency. If all of these signals are regulated away without being honored, the body eventually erupts — not because it is broken, but because **it has been polite for too long**. Healing does not always mean staying. Sometimes healing means recognizing that what you have been calling "running" was actually your body trying to protect your sovereignty. The work, then, is not to eliminate the impulse — but to finally listen to what it has been trying to say.

UNIVERSAL TIMING PATTERNS
Saturn, Neptune, Uranus, Pluto Cycles
These aren't wounds—they're initiations. Cycles of restructuring, dissolution, awakening, and death-rebirth. You don't heal them; you move through them. They're the evolutionary stages your soul agreed to before you arrived. Universal timing patterns are the cycles you cannot outrun, out-think, out-heal, or out-manifest. They're not psychological, not somatic, not karmic in the personal sense. They're cosmic initiations — unavoidable chapters that arrive with surgical precision, indifferent to your plans and deeply attuned to your evolution. These cycles show up when the universe decides you're ready, not when you feel ready. And they don't feel mystical when they arrive. They feel disruptive. Inconvenient. Disorienting. Non-negotiable.

Here's the thing people misunderstand: Universal timing doesn't express itself as a single event. It expresses itself as a season — a stretch of life where everything you normally rely on stops behaving the way it used to.

The Predetermined Evolutionary Cycles
The Soul's Non-Negotiable Initiations
No matter your chart, background, or level of consciousness, there are specific evolutionary cycles every person moves through. These cycles are not personal failures or spiritual shortcomings. They are **developmental thresholds** built into the architecture of human growth. You cannot skip them. You cannot out-heal them. You cannot manifest your way around them. What astrology gives you is **context**, not control.

SATURN RETURN (Ages 27–30)
A Saturn Return marks the end of childhood consciousness, even if you've been functioning as an adult for years. It is the moment when the scaffolding of the self you inherited or performed can no longer hold.
Saturn arrives as: limits you can no longer ignore, responsibilities you can no longer avoid, truths you can no longer rationalize away. The evolutionary purpose of a Saturn Return is simple: To pull you out of the life you built unconsciously and initiate you into the life you must build consciously.

During this period, endings accelerate. Relationships dissolve. Careers destabilize. Living situations shift. Long-held assumptions crack. This does not happen because the universe is punishing you, but because your consciousness has outgrown the container it's been living in. Saturn doesn't destroy for chaos. It prunes. It removes what was built from fantasy, fear, or conditioning so something real can take root. People experience Saturn as loss because the self that dissolves often felt familiar. But Saturn is not taking from you. It is **structuring you**. It clears the space your next identity requires. You are pushed through this threshold not because you are weak, but because maturity cannot be negotiated.

PLUTO INITIATION
The Descent Into Shadow (Pluto Square Pluto, ~Ages 35–38)
The Pluto square Pluto marks the beginning of deep karmic confrontation. Life stops responding to who you pretend to be and starts responding only to what is real. This is not about external restructuring. This is about **internal excavation**.

Pluto surfaces: shadow traits you've avoided, emotional patterns you spiritualized, control mechanisms you normalized, survival strategies that no longer work. What makes Pluto so intense is repetition. The same wounds resurface. The same dynamics replay. The same emotional reactions loop until something finally breaks through denial. Pluto does not want healing. Pluto wants **truth**. This cycle strips away the false self built for survival. It exposes where you traded authenticity for safety. It forces you to confront what has been operating unconsciously for decades. You do not negotiate with Pluto. You endure it, metabolize it, and emerge transformed. When this initiation completes, the old identity cannot be resurrected. Too much has been seen.

URANUS OPPOSITION
The Shock That Rearranges Your Life (Ages 38–42)
The Uranus Opposition is often mislabeled as a "midlife crisis," but it is actually a **midlife awakening**. Uranus brings sudden clarity, disruption, and liberation. It shocks whatever has become stagnant, constricted, or false. Structures you tolerated for stability suddenly feel unbearable. This cycle often brings: abrupt endings or breakthroughs, radical shifts in direction, sudden need for freedom, intolerance for self-betrayal. Uranus does not dismantle what is true. It dismantles what is outdated. The nervous system becomes more sensitive to misalignment. The psyche refuses to perform roles

that no longer fit. You may feel restless, electrified, or impulsively drawn toward change. This is not recklessness. It is accuracy arriving faster than the ego can prepare for. By the end of the Uranus Opposition, most people say some version of: "I can't live like that anymore." And they don't.

NEPTUNE DISSOLUTION
The Unmaking of Identity (Neptune Square Neptune, ~Ages 40–44)

Neptune's initiation is quieter — and often more confusing — than the others. Where Saturn structures and Pluto exposes, Neptune **dissolves**. It erodes identity, motivation, and certainty. What once gave meaning begins to feel hollow. Direction blurs. Desire fades. Clarity slips through your fingers. This is not depression. It is **ego dissolution**. Neptune removes: identities built on survival, roles inherited rather than chosen, fantasies that substituted for truth, spiritual bypassing disguised as faith. The hardest part of this cycle is the void. Nothing feels right, but nothing new has arrived. You cannot force meaning back into existence. Every attempt to define yourself feels exhausting or false. Neptune teaches through surrender — not romantic surrender, but the kind that happens when there is nothing left to hold onto. And then, quietly, something shifts. A softer identity begins to form. Intuition recalibrates. Meaning returns from the inside rather than the mind. You don't become someone new. You become **less defended**. Neptune doesn't give you answers. It clears the noise so the truth can emerge.

JUPITER CONJUNCT THE SUN
Identity Expansion & Reorientation (Occurs Every ~12 Years)

A Jupiter–Sun conjunction marks a **cycle of identity expansion**. Unlike Saturn, Pluto, Uranus, or Neptune, this is not an initiation through loss or collapse. It is an initiation through **growth**. And that growth cannot be reversed. When Jupiter meets the Sun, the sense of self begins to outgrow its previous container. The life you've been living may still be functional, but it starts to feel too small. Not wrong. Not broken. Just insufficient. This is one of the clearest examples of an evolutionary timing pattern where awareness does not prevent change. You can know exactly what's happening and still feel pulled forward by something larger than your current identity. Jupiter asks: "Who am I becoming now?"

Jupiter expands whatever it touches. When it conjuncts the Sun, it expands: self-concept, vision, confidence, purpose, future orientation

This is a moment when identity reorganizes around **possibility** rather than survival. You may notice: a growing dissatisfaction with old roles, a desire to take up more space, increased confidence or risk tolerance, a pull toward teaching, leading, traveling, or sharing wisdom, a sense that life wants *more* from you. This does not feel like crisis. It feels like momentum. But momentum can still be disruptive.

4 EVOLUTIONARY INTENT

Before we move into how to read your natal patterns, there is one truth you must hold: Nothing in your chart is random. Not the sign. Not the house. Not the aspects. Not the tension. Not the contradictions. Everything exists because your soul put it there. Astrology isn't describing traits — it is describing intentions. And those intentions all trace back to one source as Jeffery Wolf Green Teaches: Pluto — the Soul's unresolved desires, evolutionary momentum, and core purpose for incarnating in this lifetime. Every planetary placement in your chart, including your Nodes, is built on top of Pluto's evolutionary intent.

This is why it's important to understand not just what a placement means, but why your soul chose it. Because once you know the "why," the patterns in your chart stop feeling random or punishing. They become intelligible. They become compassionate. They become workable.

Pluto: The Souls Intent
In evolutionary astrology as JWG teaches in his book, Pluto represents: the soul, it's the core desire in which a soul choses to reincarnate to which it desires to evolve past its own conditioned history. Pluto is not trauma in the modern sense, and it is not power for its own sake. It is the gravitational center of the chart because it contains the unresolved emotional material that has followed the soul across lifetimes. Pluto is not conscious. It is **instinctual memory**. These are not habits you chose. These are survival patterns the soul *became*.
At its core, Pluto represents:
- Emotional attachments carried forward from prior lives

- Desires that once ensured survival but are now obsolete
- Unresolved wounds that were never metabolized
- Control strategies that once prevented annihilation
- The emotional state the soul is still organized around

This is why Pluto feels non-negotiable. It does not ask. It *pulls*.

Example

Pluto in Scorpio — The Soul Intent of a Generation

Pluto in Scorpio (early 1980s–mid 1990s) marks an entire generation born with a very specific evolutionary purpose: to evolve From Trauma Instinct to Embodied Truth. Most descriptions of Pluto in Scorpio reduce this placement to "intensity, transformation, shadow work." But that's the surface. The real intention is much deeper — and far more demanding. This generation did not simply inherit trauma — it embodied it. Pluto in Scorpio Souls come into life with a nervous system calibrated to: detect danger before danger appears, anticipate betrayal before trust forms, seek depth before safety, merge before boundaries, flee before they can be abandoned. This instinct is ancient. It does not come from this lifetime — it comes from lifetimes where survival depended on psychic hypervigilance, emotional penetration, and immediate energetic reading of others.

My lived experience shows this clearly: the panic when connection disappears, the confusion between intuition and fear, the reflex to run when the nervous system feels cornered, the obsession with depth, truth, and intensity, the inability to tolerate artificiality, the collapse of trust the moment communication fails. Pluto in Scorpio does not "prefer intensity." It equates intensity with safety — because only through depth can it detect the truth.

    Scorpio's work is not to eliminate fear — but to differentiate:
- trauma activation vs. genuine instinct
- projection vs. perception
- fantasy vs. psychic knowing
- pattern vs. prophecy
- escape vs. truth

    Because Scorpio subconsciously believes:
- calm = dangerous
- boredom = numbness
- stillness = vulnerability
- stability = entrapment
- presence = exposure

Scorpio will burn down its own life looking for danger that does not exist. It will flee from the very thing that could heal it. It will destroy stability to avoid emotional nakedness. Because the nervous system only recognized chaos as familiar.

Taurus North Node
The Soul Intention: Self Reliance. To Recover the Body, Restore Safety, and Anchor Consciousness Into Form Most people misunderstand Taurus as a lesson in "stability" or "material comfort." But the Taurus North Node for the Scorpio generation is something far more profound: It is the reclamation of the body after lifetimes of trauma. The Taurus intention is: embodiment, somatic safety, nervous-system repair, presence instead of dissociation, slow consistency instead of emotional compulsion, form instead of fantasies, truth that is felt, not dramatized

Taurus Teaches: Safety Is a Sensation, Not a Circumstance
My lived experience shows it perfectly: The moment my body said "do not go in this house," it was the truth instinct — not fear. The moment I left my job with certainty, it was embodiment — not escape. The moment I didn't run and instead breathed through the terror, that was Taurus healing Scorpio's wound. Taurus teaches you to trust the grounded knowing, the quiet truth, the stable instinct, the body's refusal, the subtle "yes" and "no". Not the adrenaline. Not the panic. Not the fantasy. Not the underworld narratives.

The Evolution: From Psychic Dissolution → Somatic Presence
Scorpio dissolve's identity through intensity. Taurus rebuilds identity through presence. Scorpio wants death–rebirth. Taurus wants life–continuity. Scorpio wants to merge. Taurus wants to exist. Scorpio wants truth at all costs. Taurus wants peace at all costs. Scorpio digs into others' motives. Taurus learns its own needs. Together, they create: A Soul that can feel deeply without drowning. A body that can stay present without fleeing. A heart that can love without losing itself.

Why This Matters for Decoding Your Patterns
When you begin reading the archetypes in the next section, you must remember: You are not decoding isolated traits. You are decoding the architecture of a soul in transition. Pluto explains: where your patterns began, why they feel compulsive, why you repeat them, why you resist change, why certain wounds feel

existential, why certain relationships feel fated.

The Pluto–North Node axis explains the *direction* your soul intended to move in this lifetime. It reveals why life keeps rerouting you when you try to settle, why certain desires persist long after they stop making logical sense, why stability can feel unfamiliar, and why emotional simplicity often feels strangely empty or unsatisfying. It shows why your life seems to generate turning points and crises that force choice, rather than allowing you to remain comfortable by default.

This axis is the backbone of the chart because it describes the journey itself: the movement from the emotional conditioning and survival patterns carried forward through Pluto, toward the unfamiliar terrain the soul came here to develop through the North Node. Every placement in the natal chart supports this transition. Talents, challenges, relationships, timing, and repeated themes all serve the same purpose — to pull consciousness out of what is known, compulsive, and self-protective, and into what is new, untested, and necessary for growth.

Astrology is not simply a map of personality traits; it is the symbolic blueprint of your soul's evolutionary intentions. While this book offers the language of astrology through lived experience rather than technical instruction, it rests on the assumption that you already carry a basic familiarity with planetary functions and archetypal symbolism. The work here is not introductory. It is esoteric, interpretive, and rooted in the deeper currents that shape a lifetime from beneath the surface.

Soul patterns reveal themselves in the chart through the symbols that hold tension, intensity, or unfinished emotional memory. You do not need to memorize definitions to recognize them; they are felt before they are understood, sensed before they are interpreted. The chart does not tell you what will happen — it tells you what is seeking resolution through the experiences you magnetize.

But the chart does not speak in linear logic. It speaks in archetypes.
A Moon in Pisces is not simply "sensitive"; it carries the imprint of absorption, the psychic imprint of merging with the emotional fields around you. A Pluto in Scorpio is not merely "intense"; it is initiated into the depths of transformation through crisis and truth. A Saturn

placement does not indicate punishment; it exposes where identity requires structure and mastery. To locate soul patterns in your chart, look not for the most dramatic placement, but for the placement that feels familiar — the one that resembles the emotional signature that has repeated throughout your life.

The patterns will reveal themselves in:
– the planets that trigger disproportionate reactions
– the houses where life repeatedly demands growth
– the aspects that mirror the themes you cannot escape
– the transits that time the collapse of outdated identities
– the nodes that describe your karmic trajectory

Astrology does not diagnose the soul pattern; it illuminates its architecture. It gives you a language for what your life has already been teaching you. This book uses astrology in that way — not as theory, but as lived myth. Not as prediction, but as interpretation. Not as a bypass, but as a mirror.

Why I Teach Archetypes Through the Six Polarities

Astrology is built on twelve signs, but evolution happens through six. Each axis is a polarity — two signs that exist as mirrors, opposites, and correctives for one another. You cannot understand one without understanding the other, because the psyche does not operate in isolated symbols. It oscillates. It swings. It compensates. It over-corrects.

Every pattern you live expresses itself through both ends of its axis. We don't live one sign — we pendulum between two. A wounded Scorpio instinct activates a distorted Taurus instinct. A wounded Aries instinct triggers a distorted Libra instinct. A wounded Pisces instinct collapses into a distorted Virgo instinct. And the reverse is also true. This is why you can't diagnose a pattern by looking at only one sign or one planet. The psyche isn't linear — it's rhythmic. When one side becomes overactivated, the other side becomes distorted in response. Most people think they're dealing with one archetype, but what they're actually experiencing is: a polarity pulled out of balance.

Each polarity teaches one lesson through two opposite polarities

We evolve by swinging between the extremes until the psyche finds center.

- Aries–Libra swings between losing oneself and losing one's courage.

- Taurus–Scorpio swings between clinging to safety and destroying it.
- Gemini–Sagittarius swings between too many perspectives and only one.
- Cancer–Capricorn swings between over-nurturing and over-functioning.
- Leo–Aquarius swings between self-expression and self-erasure.
- Virgo–Pisces swings between hyper-control and total dissolution.

Each polarity describes a tension the soul came to resolve, and that tension cannot be healed by working with only one sign.

Why We Oscillate Between Extremes

Because trauma, conditioning, and past-life memory don't create one behavior — they create two opposite defenses that fire under different circumstances.

For example:
- When Scorpio feels unsafe, it flees into chaos.
- When Taurus feels unsafe, it clings to stability.

Both arise from the same root wound, just expressed through opposite ends of the axis. This is why someone with Scorpio trauma can stay in a dead marriage for ten years (Taurus stagnation) and also flee their life in the middle of the night (Scorpio compulsion). It's not contradiction — it's polarity imbalance.

Polarity Is the Key to Decoding Any Soul Pattern

Working with only one sign gives you half the story. Working with the polarity shows: the wound, the compensation, the coping mechanism, the blind spot, the evolutionary intention, the precise way the pattern will show up in the body, mind, relationships, and timing.

How I Use Polarity in This Book

Each archetype is explored as a pair because:

A. Your soul does not evolve through one sign — it evolves through the tension between two.
B. You cannot heal one pole without maturing the other.
C. Your patterns make sense only when you see both the instinct and the overcorrection.
D. Your breakthroughs always occur when you integrate the polarity instead of repeating extremes.

Polarity is not opposition — it is the architecture of wholeness. And when you understand it, your entire chart suddenly becomes legible, compassionate, and coherent.

From Polarity to Pattern Mechanics

Now that you understand polarity, we need to shift how you're reading the archetypes themselves. The twelve signs are not personality descriptors. They are **functional patterns of consciousness** — specific ways the soul learns, protects itself, and evolves through experience. Each archetype carries an intention, and that intention expresses itself through **mechanics**, not traits. Traits describe how something looks. Mechanics describe how something *operates*. When people get stuck with astrology, it's because they're taught to identify with signs instead of observe how those signs function under pressure. The goal here is not to tell you "who you are," but to show you **how a pattern moves through you** — how it activates, how it defends itself, how it collapses, and how it evolves.

Each archetype exists as part of a polarity, which means it is always trying to resolve an imbalance between two instincts. One side overcorrects. The other compensates. Growth happens not by choosing one side, but by learning how to **hold the tension without splitting**.

To make this practical, each archetype will be taught through:
- its **core evolutionary intention**
- its **Two Forces of expression** (when fear or conditioning takes over)
- its **planetary mechanics** — the specific planets that activate, pressure, and evolve that archetype in your life

5 ARCHETYPAL INTENTIONS

ARCHETYPAL INTENTION

Core Intention: To initiate what has never existed before. It is the spark at the beginning of an evolutionary cycle; the moment consciousness chooses experience over memory. Wherever Aries appears, the soul is attempting something new, something untested, something not derived from the past. This is not about improvement or refinement. Aries does not evolve by perfecting what already exists. It evolves by beginning. Aries is necessary because evolution cannot occur without first movement. Before there can be growth, relationship, meaning, or mastery, something must choose to emerge. Aries represents that choice. It is the moment the soul says yes to incarnation, yes to risk, yes to stepping forward without guarantees. Aries carries the raw courage required to leave the known behind.

Yet this archetype must hold a profound paradox. The same fire that initiates evolution is also the fire that reacts to unresolved fear. The impulse to move forward and the impulse to escape can feel identical in the body. Both arrive with urgency. Both demand action. One serves destiny. The other protects an old wound.

This is the central tension Aries must learn to navigate. When action is driven by instinct, it aligns with timing and expansion. When action is driven by fear, it reenacts the past under the illusion of progress. Aries' evolutionary task is not to suppress fire, speed, or impulse, but to **refine discernment**. The soul must learn to distinguish between movement that liberates and movement that defends against remembered threat. Until that distinction is embodied, Aries repeats beginnings without completion. When it is mastered, Aries becomes true initiation: action that opens the future rather than escaping the past.

ARIES TWO FORCES

INSTINCT	FEAR
is soul-led change. It arises from alignment rather than threat. When instinct is active, the body feels energized but not panicked. There is momentum without collapse. The nervous system is alert, awake, and responsive. Action feels clean. Even when the decision is bold, it carries an internal calm. Instinct often begins quietly — a subtle inner knowing, a soft signal that says, *it's time to move*. There is no argument, no urgency, no emotional flood. The body feels open rather than braced. When Aries acts from instinct, movement creates coherence. Circumstances reorganize. Endings feel complete. Beginnings feel grounded. Even risk feels purposeful.	The body responding to an old trauma trigger. It does not arise from the present moment, but from remembered threat. Before the mind can assess what is happening, the nervous system is flooded with sensation — anger, panic, urgency, agitation. The body feels cornered. Action becomes impulsive. Aries moves not to evolve, but to discharge overwhelm. This reaction often masquerades as intuition because it is fast and forceful. Fear says *now* — but not because timing is right. Because the system believes staying equals danger

Every Aries placement is shaped by a fundamental split the soul must learn to navigate: **the difference between instinct and fear**. Both forces initiate movement. Both demand action. Both arrive with urgency in the body. Yet they originate from entirely different places and lead to radically different outcomes. Aries cannot resolve this archetype intellectually. The distinction must be learned somatically, through lived experience and bodily awareness.

One of the great confusions for Aries is that fear can feel like excitement. A surge remembers adrenaline, aliveness, intensity. For a nervous system trained through survival, panic and vitality can feel nearly identical. This is why fear-based initiation often feels convincing in the moment. The body mistakes activation for truth. A key distinction lies in sequence. Instinct arrives first as a gentle signal. If it is ignored, the body escalates. Aries then experiences a sudden internal command: *time to go now*. What began as intuitive timing becomes urgency. The soul spoke softly. The nervous system shouted.

The outcomes reveal the difference. Instinct leads to expansion, even when the path is challenging. Fear leads to repetition — the same conflicts, the same ruptures, the same abrupt exits wearing new costumes. Aries' evolution depends on learning to pause long enough to feel: Is this movement emerging from clarity, or from collapse? Only the body can answer that question.

Archetypal Patterns for Aries

Sudden Beginnings and Abrupt Endings Because Aries is wired to initiate, its life is often marked by these experiences. There is a persistent sense that something must be decided *now*. Aries frequently finds itself in situations that demand immediate action: choices made under pressure, moments framed as now or never, environments that feel tense, volatile, or combustible even when others do not experience them that way. Stillness can feel dangerous. Waiting can feel like loss of control. Life seems to push Aries forward as if pausing carries risk.

Entering Situations that feel liberating at first New jobs, Relationships, Projects, Identities — only to feel threatened once momentum slows. The beginning feels electric, destined, alive. The settling phase feels constricting. As intensity decreases, the body's alarm system activates. An internal message arises: *something is wrong, I need to move*. The cycle repeats. Excitement becomes engagement. Engagement becomes discomfort. Discomfort becomes escape. Aries often leaves just as something is about to deepen. Not because it lacks commitment, but because depth can activate the body's memory of being contained, overpowered, or erased. What looks like independence on the surface is often protection underneath.

Conflict that escalates faster than intended. Small tensions feel charged. Minor disagreements feel existential. Aries may react with force or immediacy, then feel confused afterward, wondering why the response was so intense. These moments are rarely about the present interaction. They are the nervous system responding to an old imprint that says: *if I don't assert myself now, I lose myself.* The body moves before the mind understands.

Environments that require self-definition Roles with unclear boundaries, Relationships where autonomy feels threatened, Systems that feel slow, controlling, or externally directed. Even when no one is actively restricting Aries, the *possibility* of restriction can be enough to trigger preemptive action. Freedom is reclaimed before it is actually endangered.

Over time, these patterns can create a life narrative of instability: frequent restarts, fractured timelines, intense beginnings followed by sudden exits, careers or relationships that never quite reach solidity. Others may perceive Aries as impulsive, reactive, or "too much," while internally Aries experiences itself as trying to survive. People may say, "You didn't have to leave," not realizing that Aries' body experienced the moment as a threshold between safety and annihilation.

Until the distinction between trauma and truth becomes conscious, Aries may take action again and again, mistaking urgency for intuition. The repetition is not failure. It is the psyche insisting on awareness. The pattern continues until action no longer serves fragmentation, but integration.

Early Experiences for Aries
In early life, Aries often learns its core survival strategy through a moment when instinct could not be acted upon or was not trusted. There may have been a time when the body registered danger, urgency, or the need to move — and yet movement was impossible, discouraged, or punished. Or instinct may have been overridden by authority, circumstance, or fear. The nervous system learned a critical lesson: **waiting is unsafe**. From this imprint, a single belief takes root in the body long before it becomes conscious: *If I don't act, I'm not safe.* Action becomes synonymous with survival. Movement becomes regulation. Stillness begins to feel like exposure.

This early learning creates a reflexive pattern. Aries becomes highly sensitive to perceived threat and responds preemptively. There is a tendency to flee before danger is confirmed, to assert independence before it is challenged, to defend autonomy before anyone has attempted to take it. Intensity is interpreted as risk. Containment feels like control. Pausing feels like surrender.

Because the body learned that safety depended on speed, Aries grows accustomed to acting before understanding. The nervous system reacts first. The mind arrives later. Movement replaces discernment. Choosing stillness feels far more dangerous than choosing motion, even when no real threat is present.

These early imprints are not flaws. They are adaptive responses formed in conditions where waiting, trusting, or remaining present did not feel viable. The problem is not the instinct to move. The challenge arises when that instinct continues to operate long after the original danger has passed. Aries' evolutionary work begins when the body learns that action can be chosen — not compelled — and that instinct can guide without urgency.

Core Lessons for Aries

The central lesson Aries must consciously learn is the **somatic distinction between anxiety and excitement**. Both activate the body. Both generate urgency. Both can feel like readiness. Yet they lead in opposite directions. Anxiety pulls the soul back toward the past, reenacting unfinished survival responses. Excitement carries the soul forward into a life that has not yet existed. The body knows the difference, but only through awareness and repetition.

Aries evolves by learning to pause inside activation rather than obey it. The question is not whether to act, but **why**. Is this response emerging from present-moment truth, or from a remembered threat? When Aries learns to ask, *Is this danger now, or danger then?* the fire begins to mature. Anger no longer leads. It becomes information. Urgency gives way to courage. Action becomes chosen rather than automatic.

The soul does not ask Aries to suppress instinct or soften its fire. Fire is sacred. It is the force of becoming. What must change is the source of ignition. Fear-driven action fragments. Truth-driven action organizes reality. Aries learns through lived experience that when movement is aligned with intuition and expansion, life responds. Circumstances rearrange. Resistance dissolves. Reality submits not through force, but through coherence.

The deeper wisdom hidden inside repeated failed attempts is this: **alignment is more powerful than speed**. When Aries acts from clarity, it does not need to fight for space. Space opens. When Aries stays because staying is safe, depth becomes possible. When Aries leaves, it is not to escape discomfort, but because a cycle is complete. True instinct arrives quietly, without argument or adrenaline. It does not shout. It does not collapse the body. Aries becomes whole when courage protects the future, not the wound — when fire initiates life rather than defends against memory.

The Polarity Path: Libra
Libra teaches Aries that existence does not require opposition. Desire does not require domination. Independence does not require isolation. Strength does not require constant motion. Leadership does not require winning. These are not moral lessons. They are nervous system truths. Aries learns through Libra that pausing does not erase the self. It refines it.

For Aries, relationship can initially feel like threat. Feedback can feel like control. Dialogue can feel like delay. Yet over time, a deeper truth emerges: many moments of reactive action could have been avoided if reflection had been allowed in. Advice was not always an attempt to dominate. Slowness was not always an attempt to stop momentum. Often, it was simply perspective trying to enter the room.

Libra shows Aries that choice made in dialogue is not weakness, but precision. That power does not vanish when it listens. That instinct matures when it is mirrored rather than obeyed blindly. When Aries allows another presence to reflect its impulse, the body relaxes. The nervous system no longer has to fight for space or prove its right to exist.
Through Libra, Aries learns that stillness can hold strength, and consideration can sharpen intention. Action becomes more exact. Timing becomes cleaner. Movement no longer needs to announce itself through urgency.

The evolutionary arc completes when Aries no longer needs to stand alone in order to be real. Action ceases to be a reaction against imagined threat and becomes a conscious offering to life. In this integration, fire does not diminish — it steadies. And when it moves, it does so with purpose, clarity, and shared reality.

LIBRA
ARCHETYPAL INTENTION

Core Intention: Learning Truth in Relationship Without Trading Yourself for Stability. To restore balance where relationship and selfhood have fallen out of alignment across lifetimes. Wherever Libra appears, the soul is attempting to correct a relational imbalance that was once survived through compromise, appeasement, or self-silencing. This is not about learning how to be agreeable. It is about learning how to remain *true* while in relationship.

Libra is necessary in the evolutionary cycle because nature itself requires balance in order to sustain life. Consciousness cannot evolve in isolation forever, nor can it mature through union that erases the self. Libra introduces the next essential lesson after initiation: how to meet the other without abandoning oneself. The soul must learn to stop sacrificing its needs, desires, and truths in exchange for safety, stability, or belonging. Without this lesson, relationship becomes a place of quiet loss rather than mutual growth.

Archetypally, Libra governs the space *between* two beings. It is the field where attraction, reflection, and reciprocity occur. Through Libra, the soul learns how it gives, how it receives, and what it believes it must trade in order to be loved. The deeper intention is not harmony at any cost, but **justice within relationship** — the restoration of equity between self and other.

The paradox Libra must hold is profound. It carries both the need for connection and the need for autonomy. It longs for union, yet cannot evolve through merger that requires self-erasure. It seeks peace, yet cannot mature by avoiding conflict. Libra must learn that relationship does not require the abandonment of truth, and that autonomy does not require separation.

Until this tension is consciously embodied, Libra oscillates between attachment and resentment. When integrated, Libra becomes the archetype of relational integrity: the ability to remain open, connected, and loving without disappearing. In this balance, the soul discovers that harmony is not the absence of disruption, but the presence of truth held with care.

LIBRA TWO FORCES

RELATIONSHIP	SELF RETREAT
There comes a point where Libra no longer knows how to remain connected without losing itself. Needs go unspoken. Desires are deferred. Truth is delayed in service of harmony. The body begins to register imbalance long before the mind can name it. Energy turns inward. Libra retreats internally, moving into the Taurus function of self-containment. Somatically, this can feel like heaviness, depression, anger, or resentment. Nothing is "wrong" on the surface, yet something essential feels compromised. Because Libra is relationally oriented, this inward turn can feel like failure or emotional shutdown. The soul senses imbalance but does not yet understand its source. When this discomfort is misunderstood, Libra may externalize it. The partner becomes the perceived problem. Relationship feels restrictive. The nervous system seeks relief through separation, often activating the Aries polarity. Libra leaves not from clarity, but from accumulated self-abandonment. The exit brings temporary relief, followed by a deeper confusion: Why do I feel just as empty now?	When Libra is without a mirror, loneliness sets in. The same emotional states appear — sadness, anger, grief, longing. The body again signals imbalance. But this time, the absence of relationship is interpreted as the wound. Libra looks back and wonders why it left. The ache for connection intensifies. The soul is not punishing Libra. It is teaching discernment. Both forces feel the same somatically. Depression, heaviness, sadness, resentment. One arises from losing yourself in relationship. The other arises from losing relationship entirely. Without awareness, Libra oscillates between the two, mistaking emotional pain for proof that something external must change.

Every Libra placement must navigate a subtle but painful split: **the need for relationship versus the need to preserve the self**. Both forces are legitimate. Both arise from the same desire for balance. And both can feel nearly identical in the body — which is why Libra so often becomes confused about what is actually wrong.

The lesson is not moral. It is somatic. Libra must learn to **relate inwardly before relating outwardly**. These feelings are Venusian signals, not failures. They point toward an unfinished relationship with the self. When Libra learns to tend to its own values, desires, and worth internally, the polarity resolves. Relationship no longer requires self-erasure. Aloneness no longer feels like abandonment. Only then can Libra embody Venus fully — attracting partners whose values align with its soul, rather than using relationship to compensate for an unclaimed self.

Archetypal Patterns Libra

Libra unconsciously creates recurring life situations through oscillation. When the core lesson of balance has not yet been integrated, the psyche moves back and forth between the Libra and Aries poles, attempting to resolve imbalance through extremes rather than embodiment. Because this movement happens below conscious awareness, Libra often believes circumstances or partners are the problem, when in truth the pattern itself is seeking correction.

One common Libra pattern begins with **self-suppression in the name of harmony**. Truth is delayed. Needs are minimized. Desire is negotiated away for the sake of peace. Libra adapts, accommodates, and reassures itself that stability matters more than authenticity. Over time, the cost of this suppression accumulates in the body as resentment, anger, and emotional fatigue. Eventually, Libra reaches an internal breaking point. What follows can feel sudden or dramatic: *I am done*. The relationship ends abruptly, often surprising the other person, who experienced the bond as stable or functional. From the outside, the ending looks impulsive. From the inside, it feels overdue by years.

Another variation of this pattern involves **domineering dynamics**. Libra may find itself in relationships where the partner's needs, emotions, or authority dominate the field. Libra loses itself by over-accommodating, becoming dependent on the relationship for identity, validation, or direction. Less commonly, Libra swings to the opposite extreme and becomes the dominating force — controlling harmony, dictating emotional tone, or managing the relationship to avoid disruption. In both cases, balance is lost. One self expands while the other contracts.

A particularly painful pattern arises when **needs are fulfilled asymmetrically**. One partner feels complete, while the other feels abandoned or confused. Libra may leave once its unspoken needs are finally met or clarified, even though the other partner believes the relationship is still viable. Or Libra may be the one left behind, wondering how something that felt "balanced" could end. In either case, the imbalance demands replay. The karma is not punishment — it is unfinished learning. The soul repeats the scenario until equality is consciously restored.

Another recurring situation involves **mutual dependency**. Both partners rely heavily on each other for emotional regulation, meaning, or stability. The relationship becomes the container for identity itself. Growth slows. Individual becoming is sacrificed to maintain closeness. Over time, stagnation sets in. Frustration builds. Confrontation becomes inevitable, either externally through conflict or internally through dissatisfaction and withdrawal.

All of these patterns serve the same purpose: to enforce **relational equality, balance, and relativity**. Libra is being taught that both partners' needs, desires, and truths are equally meaningful. Over-giving and over-receiving are equally destabilizing. Losing yourself to maintain harmony is no more balanced than severing relationship to reclaim autonomy.

These situations inevitably create confrontation — with the partner, with guilt, with loneliness, or with the self. That confrontation is the mirror Libra needs. It forces reflection, examination, and recalibration. Through repetition, Libra learns how to give without erasing, how to receive without dependence, and how to remain present without dominating or disappearing.

The archetype is not asking Libra to choose relationship over self, or self over relationship. It is asking Libra to stop swinging between extremes and learn how to **inhabit the middle** — where love can move freely, and both souls are allowed to grow.

Early Experiences Libra

Libra's survival strategy is learned early through observation, not instruction. As a child, Libra often witnesses relational dynamics where balance is missing. One parent may over give while the other's needs consistently take precedence. Love appears conditional. Stability seems to depend on accommodation. The child learns, without being told, that harmony is preserved by minimizing disruption and managing the emotional field.

In some cases, Libra observes self-erasure modeled as virtue. Sacrifice is praised. Endurance is rewarded. Wanting more is framed as selfish or ungrateful. In others, the child encounters the opposite extreme: a parent who is overly Aries in nature — dominant, reactive, or self-directed — whose intensity overwhelms the relational space. In response, Libra unconsciously takes a vow in the opposite direction: *I will not be like that.* Peace becomes the identity. Adaptation becomes safety.

When Libra does attempt to express Aries qualities — anger, desire, autonomy, directness — those expressions may be judged, corrected, or subtly discouraged. The body learns that assertion threatens connection. The nervous system registers disapproval faster than the mind can interpret it. Over time, Libra's system associates self-expression with risk and relational harmony with survival.

These imprints are not flaws. They are intelligent adaptations to an environment where balance did not exist naturally. The child learns to read the room, anticipate needs, and regulate others emotionally because that skill keeps connection intact. The body learns long before the mind does that staying connected requires adjustment.

The challenge arises when this early strategy persists into adulthood, long after the original conditions have changed. What once protected belonging now suppresses truth. Libra's evolutionary work begins when the body learns that relationship can survive honesty — and that balance does not require disappearance.

Core Lessons for Libra

The central lesson Libra must consciously learn is **how to recognize and respond to imbalance without abandoning either the relationship or the self**. Libra is not here to avoid conflict or maintain peace at all costs. It is here to understand *why* imbalance arises and *how* it moves through the body and psyche when it does.

Through repeated relational patterns, Libra is asked to develop awareness of its automatic responses to imbalance: self-silencing, over-accommodation, withdrawal, or sudden severing. These responses are not random. They are inherited, learned, and reinforced through early experience. The wisdom emerges when Libra begins to observe these patterns rather than identify with them. *What am I trying to protect right now? What am I afraid will happen if I tell the truth?*

A core aspect of Libra's evolution is the development of **inner worth that is not dependent on external validation or relational stability**. This is the Taurus function maturing within. Libra must learn to anchor value internally so that care for the other does not require self-erasure. When worth is embodied inwardly, relationship becomes a choice rather than a necessity for survival.

Libra also learns discernment. Not every relationship dynamic is healthy simply because it is familiar. The soul must learn to distinguish dysfunctional patterns inherited from family or culture from relationships rooted in mutual respect. Equality becomes the guiding principle: both voices matter, both needs deserve space, both truths belong.

When imbalance occurs, the lesson is not to flee or endure silently, but to **name the imbalance and correct it**. Correction may come through honest conversation, boundary-setting, renegotiation, or, when necessary, conscious separation. Libra matures when it understands that justice in relationship begins within — and that restoring balance is an act of love, not disruption.

The Polarity Path: Aries

Aries does not arrive to disrupt relationship for its own sake. It arrives to reintroduce truth, movement, and initiation where balance has become stagnant. Through Aries, Libra learns that evolution within relationship cannot be negotiated into existence. It must be initiated.
Aries teaches Libra how to recognize when a new evolutionary cycle is required. There comes a moment in every relationship when the existing structure can no longer support what is becoming. This moment is not always logical. It is felt. Aries brings Libra back into contact with that inner knowing. Desire does not require consensus. Truth does not need approval. Wanting more does not make you selfish. These are not threats to relationship — they are signals of life seeking expression.

Through Aries, Libra learns that conflict does not equal loss. Disruption does not automatically mean abandonment. Separation is not betrayal when it arises from alignment rather than avoidance. Aries shows Libra that choosing yourself is not an act against the other. It is an act of fidelity to life itself.
Balance does not occur through suppression. It occurs through **relationship that allows movement**. Aries teaches Libra that action can clarify what endless deliberation obscures. Movement reveals truth faster than negotiation. When something is spoken, initiated, or acted upon, reality responds. Stagnation dissolves. Clarity emerges.

As Libra integrates Aries, it learns to bring decisive action into relationship without severing connection. Boundaries are named. Truth is spoken earlier. Desire is honored before resentment accumulates. Libra no longer waits until self-erasure becomes unbearable. It initiates adjustment while relationship is still alive. Libra's evolution completes when it stops asking who might be disappointed and starts honoring what is alive within. In this integration, Libra does not lose its capacity for care or fairness. It gains vitality. Relationship becomes a space where both souls can move, change, and grow — without one disappearing so the other can remain.

TAURUS

ARCHETYPAL INTENTION

Core Intention: To build safety through embodiment and inner self reliance. It is the archetype that teaches consciousness how to remain present in form. After Aries initiates life and movement, Taurus must answer a critical question: Can the soul stay here? Can it inhabit the body, tolerate sensation, and create stability without grasping, clinging, or freezing in fear?

Taurus is necessary in the evolutionary cycle because initiation alone is not enough. What is begun must be held. What is sparked must be sustained. Taurus slows consciousness down so it can root into matter, rhythm, and reality. It teaches how to stay, how to build, how to endure — not through force or control, but through grounded presence. Without Taurus, life becomes a series of unfinished beginnings. With Taurus, experience gains weight, continuity, and coherence.

The deeper intention of Taurus is to teach internal self-reliance. Safety is not meant to come from people, possessions, routines, or predictability. Those are external supports, not sources. Taurus teaches the soul how to feel secure inside the body itself — how to remain present with sensation, discomfort, pleasure, and need without abandoning oneself or reaching outward for regulation. This is embodiment, not as a concept, but as a nervous system capacity.

At the heart of Taurus is a paradox. The same instinct that creates stability can also imprison the soul in familiar suffering. What grounds can also stagnate. What provides comfort can quietly erode vitality. Taurus must learn the difference between security, which nourishes life, and comfort, which merely preserves it.

The evolutionary task is not to reject stability, but to refine it. Taurus matures when safety no longer depends on sameness, and when stability becomes a foundation for growth rather than a barrier to change. When embodied, Taurus becomes the place where life can truly live — steadily, sensually, and sustainably.

TAURUS TWO FORCES

EMBODIMENT	RESISTANCE
This is the capacity to stay present with sensation as life begins to shift internally. Embodiment does not rush change, but it does not deny it. When embodiment is active, the body becomes an instrument of truth. Signals arise quietly at first: a subtle loss of pleasure, a heaviness where there was once ease, a sense that something no longer fits. These sensations are not dramatic. They are coherent. The nervous system is not panicked, but attentive. Over time, clarity consolidates. The body reaches a point of readiness — much like labor — where movement is no longer optional. Change is not forced. It is birthed. When Taurus embodies change, the transition feels inevitable rather than frightening. Stability reorganizes instead of collapsing.	the fear-based response to the same internal signals. Resistance arises when comfort is mistaken for security. Life may look good externally: routines are established, resources are steady, relationships are predictable. There is little overt conflict. Yet internally, a quiet dissatisfaction grows. Something feels missing. Because Taurus is oriented toward continuity, the instinct is to stay, to preserve what works, to avoid disruption. The body's early signals are ignored or normalized. As resistance continues, the body begins to compensate. Sensation dulls. Energy thickens. Taurus often describes this as hitting a wall — an internal sense of heaviness, inertia, or stuckness that makes forward movement feel impossible. This wall is not punishment. It is the body's last attempt to prevent further self-betrayal. The nervous system refuses to carry a life that no longer aligns with truth.

Every Taurus placement must navigate a fundamental split: **the choice between embodying change and resisting it**. Both forces arise from the same desire for safety. Both can look calm, stable, and grounded on the surface. And both are felt primarily in the body, not the mind. The difference is not moral. It is somatic.

Crucially, **embodiment and resistance can feel very similar at first**. Both are slow. Both are quiet. Both involve staying. The difference lies in vitality. Embodiment feels alive, even when it is uncomfortable. There is presence in the sensation. Resistance feels numbing. The body feels muted, dulled, or burdened. One expands awareness. The other contracts it.

When Taurus resists change, life does not fall apart immediately. Instead, meaning drains away. Pleasure fades. Desire goes dormant. When Taurus embodies change, discomfort may increase temporarily, but coherence returns. Energy flows again. The body feels truthful.

The lesson Taurus must learn is not *when* to change, but **how to listen**. The body always knows first. When Taurus trusts that knowledge, stability becomes a living foundation. When it resists, stability becomes a cage.

Archetypal Patterns Taurus

Taurus unconsciously creates recurring life situations through endurance. When the archetypal lesson of embodiment has not yet been integrated, Taurus equates staying with safety and leaving with collapse. As a result, life repeatedly places Taurus in circumstances that feel *stable enough to remain in*, yet costly enough to slowly erode vitality. These situations are not overtly harmful. They are tolerable. And that is precisely what allows the pattern to persist.

There is often a specific area of life where Taurus holds on tightly even as something essential is fading. Jobs, relationships, homes, identities. The internal logic is simple and compelling: *I've already put so much into this. It has to pay off.* Time, effort, loyalty, and care become reasons to stay, even when the soul has finished growing. Taurus does not leave because something explodes. It stays because nothing does.

A defining Taurus pattern is remaining long past the point of nourishment. Situations decay slowly rather than ending cleanly. Discomfort accumulates first in the body. Fatigue replaces enthusiasm. Heaviness replaces ease. Desire goes quiet. Sensation dulls. Meanwhile, the mind reassures itself: *This is fine. This is stable. This is safer than the unknown.* Taurus often requires the body to become loud before permission to change is granted.

Another recurring Taurus scene involves **over-investment**. Taurus pours loyalty, labor, time, and emotional energy into people and structures with the expectation that endurance will eventually be rewarded with security. When that security does not arrive, Taurus does not withdraw. It commits harder. The reasoning becomes circular: *I can't leave now. I've already given too much.* Attachment tightens not from greed or stubbornness, but from fear of losing what has been built.

Taurus also becomes familiar with **tolerable suffering**. Relationships that are emotionally muted but dependable. Work that is uninspiring but reliable. Lives that function smoothly on the surface while quietly starving the soul underneath. Because Taurus equates safety with continuity, dissatisfaction is normalized. Desire is postponed. Fulfillment is deferred. Grief is held silently in the body, often without language.

Another pattern appears when opportunity calls for change. A new path requires risk, flexibility, or temporary instability. The body registers readiness, but the mind hesitates. Taurus waits. The moment passes. Later, resentment surfaces — not toward others, but toward the self for not moving when the body first knew it was time.

When the Taurus pattern finally reaches its limit, the collapse is rarely dramatic. It is somatic. Energy drains. Motivation disappears. The body simply refuses to continue. What looks like depression, burnout, or inertia is often the nervous system declining to carry a life that no longer supports the soul.

Early Experiences Taurus

Taurus learns its survival strategy early, often in environments where stability could not be relied upon externally. In the early years, Taurus may have been required — subtly or overtly — to take care of itself. Needs may not have been consistently met. Safety may have felt conditional or unpredictable. As a result, the child learned to generate steadiness from within. Self-reliance became not a preference, but a necessity. From this environment, a core bodily belief forms: *I survive by creating stability.* The nervous system learns this long before the mind can articulate it. The body associates continuity with safety and disruption with danger. Staying becomes regulation. Endurance becomes proof of strength. Taurus learns to hold, to manage, to conserve — because these behaviors keep life intact.

This imprint is adaptive. It is not a flaw. When leaving, risking, or depending on others felt unsafe, the body learned to anchor itself. Taurus developed patience, resilience, and the capacity to endure discomfort without collapse. These traits allowed survival in conditions where instability would have been overwhelming.

The challenge arises when this early strategy continues long after it is needed. When Taurus is wounded or unbalanced, the same survival response repeats: **you stay**. Long after the soul has outgrown the situation. Long after the body has begun to shut down. Long after comfort has decayed into numbness. The nervous system interprets uncertainty as annihilation, even when the present moment no longer holds real threat. This creates patterns of over-attachment to people, environments, and routines. Fear of scarcity — emotional or financial — intensifies. Dependence on external structures for security increases, even as vitality decreases. Leaving feels like collapse, not choice.

Taurus' work is not to abandon its instinct for stability, but to update it. The body must learn that safety can exist inside change, and that self-reliance does not require staying where life has already moved on.

Core Lessons Taurus

The central lesson Taurus must consciously learn is **how to listen to the body before it reaches breaking point**. Taurus is not here to abandon stability, but to refine it. The soul asks Taurus to distinguish between stability that nourishes life and stability that quietly traps it. This distinction is not conceptual. It is somatic.

Through repeated experiences of staying long past expiration — in jobs, relationships, identities, and routines — Taurus learns the subtle language of the body. Early signals are gentle: a loss of pleasure, a dulling of desire, a heaviness where there was once ease. When these signals are ignored, the body escalates. Fatigue deepens. Motivation disappears. Eventually, collapse forces what awareness could have chosen earlier. The wisdom emerges when Taurus recognizes this pattern and begins to trust the whisper instead of waiting for the scream.

Taurus must learn to honor discomfort as information rather than threat. Change does not mean failure. Uncertainty does not mean danger. Letting go of comfort that costs the future is not loss — it is preservation of life force. The soul does not ask Taurus to rush or force transformation. It asks for responsiveness. When the body signals readiness, movement can be slow, steady, and grounded — but it must happen.

A key aspect of Taurus' evolution is learning that **safety can exist inside change**. Stability does not have to be permanent to be real. Security does not require sameness. As Taurus embodies this truth, self-reliance deepens rather than collapses. The language Taurus learns to work with is simple and direct: *Is this nourishing me? Has this completed its purpose? Am I staying from truth or from fear?* Taurus becomes whole when stability supports evolution — when comfort becomes a foundation rather than a cage, and the body is trusted as the most reliable guide forward.

The Polarity Path: Scorpio

Scorpio does not come to destroy what Taurus has built. It comes to reveal what is no longer alive. Through Scorpio, Taurus learns that truth and authenticity must exist *inside* stability, not outside of it.

Scorpio teaches Taurus that safety does not come from holding on. Stability does not require permanence. Loss is not annihilation. Change is not betrayal. Depth is not danger. These lessons are not intellectual. They are lived through surrender. Scorpio asks Taurus to trust what happens when control is loosened and attachment is released. What decays must be allowed to die so that something real can regenerate.

For Taurus, this is deeply confronting. The instinct to preserve is strong. Letting go can feel like disappearance. Yet Scorpio reveals a different kind of security — one that arises from resilience rather than continuity. Through transformation, Taurus discovers that it does not vanish when something ends. It remains. In fact, it becomes more itself.

Scorpio introduces Taurus to emotional and energetic truth. Where Taurus seeks comfort, Scorpio seeks depth. Where Taurus holds steady, Scorpio moves inward. This movement teaches Taurus that sensation can be survived, intensity can be tolerated, and endings can be integrated without collapse. The body learns that it can remain present even as form changes.

As Taurus integrates Scorpio, stability becomes dynamic rather than static. Self-reliance no longer depends on what is being held. Trust shifts from external structures to inner capacity. Change stops feeling like threat and begins to feel like renewal. Taurus' evolution completes when it no longer equates safety with sameness. Through Scorpio, it learns to trust itself through loss, transition, and transformation — knowing that what is essential cannot be taken, and what must end does so in service of life continuing.

SCORPIO
ARCHETYPAL INTENTION

Core Intention: To confront limitation in order to transmute it. This archetype governs the descent into the places where consciousness has been fractured by trauma, powerlessness, betrayal, or loss. Scorpio is where the soul must face what it has avoided, buried, or survived by dissociation. Its purpose is not suffering for its own sake, but revelation — uncovering *why* a pattern exists so it can finally be released.

Scorpio is necessary in the evolutionary cycle because wholeness cannot be achieved without shadow integration. Growth does not come only from building or stabilizing; it also requires excavation. The soul must confront its emotional attachments, survival strategies, and inherited wounds in order to reclaim lost power. Scorpio teaches the difference between **trauma-driven instinct** and **truth-driven instinct** — a distinction that determines whether intensity becomes healing or harm.

At its core, Scorpio's intention is to evolve through truth rather than trauma. It governs elimination, regeneration, emotional intimacy, death of identity, and the underworld of the psyche where unresolved karmic memory lives. Scorpio senses what is hidden, unspoken, or unresolved, often before others are aware anything exists. This sensitivity is both its gift and its challenge.

The paradox Scorpio must hold is profound. Scorpio feels most alive when something is ending. Collapse, disruption, and revelation bring intensity that feels like vitality. As a result, Scorpio can become obsessed with investigating shadows, exposing motives, or dismantling structures — sometimes endlessly destroying without allowing new life to begin. On the other end of the spectrum, Scorpio may resist beginning anything at all, unconsciously waiting for inevitable loss.

The same instinct that leads to transformation can also lead to self-destruction. The same emotional depth that detects truth can also hallucinate threat where none exists. Scorpio's evolutionary task is to discern whether its impulse arises from present-moment truth or unresolved wounding. When this distinction is embodied, Scorpio becomes the alchemist of the zodiac — capable of turning pain into power, endings into rebirth, and shadow into integrated wholeness.

Every Scorpio placement is shaped by a fundamental split: **the drive to evolve through truth versus the compulsion to repeat trauma in the name of survival**. Scorpio correlates with the soul itself and the principle of evolution. It is where consciousness becomes aware of forces larger than the personal self and feels the urge to merge with them in order to grow, transform, and reclaim power. This archetype pulls awareness toward depth, intensity, and the bottom line of experience.

SCORPIO TWO FORCES

TRUTH	TRAUMA
the soul-aligned impulse toward evolution. Truth instinct is not comfortable, but it is coherent. It drives Scorpio to penetrate beneath appearances, to ask why, and to confront both the brightest and darkest aspects of the self without flinching. Somatically, truth instinct feels intense but grounded. The body is activated without being frantic. There is focus rather than obsession. Pain may arise, but it carries meaning. Scorpio senses where growth is required and commits to transformation — releasing emotional attachments, outdated behaviors, and unconscious loyalties that inhibit evolution. This force allows Scorpio to merge with power without becoming dependent on it. Change is chosen. Metamorphosis is self-	the fear-based imitation of evolution. Trauma instinct feels urgent, compulsive, and emotionally charged. It arises from unresolved memories of abandonment, betrayal, loss, or powerlessness. Scorpio still seeks depth and intensity, but now as regulation rather than truth. The body feels contracted, hypervigilant, and defensive. Obsession replaces curiosity. Control replaces surrender. Scorpio becomes over-invested emotionally in people, patterns, or sources of power that promise safety or dominance. Compulsions form. Dynamics stagnate even as intensity escalates.

directed.

Both forces feel similar at first. Both are intense. Both demand depth. Both pull Scorpio beneath the surface of life. The difference is revealed in outcome and embodiment. Truth instinct leads to release, regeneration, and increased self-reliance. Trauma instinct leads to fixation, repetition, and dependency. One integrates shadow. The other becomes trapped inside it.

At its most integrated, Scorpio motivates growth in others without manipulation and confronts its own limitations without outsourcing power. At its most distorted, Scorpio attempts to control evolution rather than submit to it. The lesson is not to avoid intensity, but to discern **why** it is being pursued. Scorpio evolves when it learns to feel the difference between power that liberates and power that protects an old wound — and chooses truth even when trauma feels louder.

Archetypal Patterns Scorpio

Wherever Scorpio appears, life repeatedly places the soul inside situations that feel intense, fated, and terminal. Relationships, identities, careers, and inner landscapes often feel as though they are approaching an ending — even when nothing external is actually collapsing. Scorpio lives with the embodied sensation that *something must die in order for something else to live*. This perception is not imagined. It is archetypal. The challenge is how that perception is acted upon.

Scorpio becomes acutely aware that evolution is required. It senses stagnation, emotional falseness, and unresolved undercurrents long before others do. This awareness creates a split. One path leads toward integration and conscious transmutation. The other leads toward resistance, control, and repetition. Both paths feel intense in the body. Both feel urgent. Both feel necessary.

A defining Scorpio pattern emerges when **destruction is initiated in the name of transformation**. When trauma instinct is active, intensity becomes synonymous with truth. Scorpio feels pressure to cut, sever, expose, or dismantle — not because the situation is irredeemable, but because the nervous system cannot tolerate the tension of waiting. Relationships may end abruptly. Confrontations may escalate sharply. Structures are dismantled prematurely. The body experiences temporary relief, followed by exhaustion. Nothing is allowed to stabilize. Just as something begins to root, the familiar internal signal arises: *this can't last*. Over time, Scorpio grows fatigued — not because transformation is wrong, but because it is being forced rather than integrated.

Another recurring Scorpio pattern is **emotional fusion followed by rupture**. Scorpio bonds deeply and quickly, often sensing karmic familiarity or soul-level recognition. Attachment forms at a cellular level. Once bonded, trauma instinct activates vigilance. Small shifts are read as betrayal. Distance feels like abandonment. Neutrality feels dangerous. The body tightens. Scorpio may unconsciously test others — intensifying, withdrawing, probing — until the relationship collapses under the weight of unspoken fear. What Scorpio experiences as self-protection often appears as sabotage to others.

Scorpio also repeatedly encounters **power struggles**, even when power was never consciously sought. Others may project control, suspicion, or intensity onto Scorpio, reinforcing the belief that closeness equals danger. These dynamics become self-confirming: intimacy feels unsafe, so defenses rise, which then provoke exposure.

A quieter but equally destabilizing pattern is **identity death without regeneration**. Scorpio sheds skins frequently — roles, relationships, self-concepts — but may not allow enough time for rebirth. The psyche becomes accustomed to liminal space: no longer who you were, not yet who you are becoming. Grief accumulates without closure. Life feels perpetually unresolved.

Early Experiences Scorpio

Scorpio's survival strategy forms early through experiences where safety is suddenly removed. There may have been moments of abandonment, betrayal, emotional rupture, or loss where the ground disappeared without warning. What was trusted vanished. What felt secure proved unreliable. From these experiences, the nervous system learned a single, overriding rule: **danger comes without notice**.

In response, Scorpio learned that survival depends on detection. If truth can be uncovered early enough — if motives are exposed, intentions investigated, emotional shifts tracked — then loss can be anticipated and power reclaimed. This strategy is not taught. It is embodied. The body becomes hyper-attuned to emotional undercurrents long before the mind can name them.

This imprint is adaptive, not flawed. Expecting betrayal before love and abandonment before presence once made sense. Protecting the heart before anyone approaches it prevented deeper injury. Scorpio internalizes one core belief at a cellular level: *If I am not vigilant, I will be destroyed*. This script is often karmic — carried across lifetimes — and activated early through circumstance rather than choice.

Over time, fear is projected outward. Emotional perception intensifies. Scorpio may begin to see meaning where none exists, reading between the lines constantly. Fusion with others occurs quickly, followed by sudden withdrawal when threat is perceived. People may be tested unconsciously to determine whether they are safe. Neutrality feels like rejection. Silence feels loaded. The nervous system oscillates between closeness and defense.

When triggered, Scorpio may shut down completely or erupt with intensity. This is not sabotage by intent. It is protection by reflex. The body moves faster than awareness. What appears controlling or extreme from the outside is, internally, an attempt to prevent annihilation. Scorpio's evolutionary work begins when the nervous system learns that presence can exist without threat — and that truth does not need to be hunted in order to be real.

Core Lessons Scorpio
As Scorpio learns to distinguish truth instinct from trauma instinct, these situations soften without becoming shallow. Scorpio no longer needs to end things to feel alive. Intensity becomes grounded. Depth becomes sustainable. Relationships stop reenacting past-life betrayals and begin supporting present intimacy. Transformation still happens — but it happens internally first. Scorpio learns that not everything false needs to be burned; some things can simply be outgrown. Endings become conscious instead of catastrophic. Regeneration replaces exhaustion. Scorpio matures when: your emotional body becomes coherent: your intuition becomes accurate, your relationships stop reenacting past-life trauma, you trust without needing evidence, you let the old identities die without dragging others into the fire.

The Polarity Path: Taurus
Taurus teaches Scorpio how to remain alive without being in crisis. Where Scorpio seeks truth through intensity, Taurus offers truth through continuity. Where Scorpio trusts transformation through dismantling, Taurus reveals that growth can occur through steadiness.

Taurus teaches Scorpio that not every truth requires destruction. Not every ending is necessary. Depth does not have to hurt in order to be real. Stability is not stagnation. Staying is not weakness. What is authentic does not need to be tested through suffering or forced collapse. Security can be built slowly, patiently, through lived experience rather than emotional extremes.

For Scorpio, this lesson is profound. The nervous system has learned to associate aliveness with intensity and safety with vigilance. Taurus introduces a different somatic reality. The body learns that peace can be tolerated. Calm does not mean danger. Nothing terrible happens when things remain intact. Over time, trust grows not through exposure to threat, but through consistency.

This does not mean Scorpio abandons transformation. It means transformation becomes **integrated rather than violent**. Taurus reminds Scorpio that regeneration requires something to remain. Roots must exist for depth to sustain itself. Without this grounding, Scorpio burns through identities, relationships, and inner worlds without ever arriving at rest.

At times, when Scorpio clings to intensity or control, life may indeed pull the rug out — not as punishment, but as redirection. These moments force Scorpio back into Taurus' lesson of self-reliance: learning to stabilize internally rather than gripping external power or emotional fusion. Collapse occurs only when peace has been refused. Scorpio's evolution completes when it no longer equates transformation with suffering. When it learns that truth can unfold gently. When it allows peace to be enough. In Taurus, Scorpio discovers that what is real does not need to be destroyed to be trusted — it only needs to be lived.

ARCHETYPAL INTENTION

Core Intention: To know reality through connection. This archetype carries an inherent desire to understand life intellectually — not in isolation, but through exchange. Gemini learns by observing, naming, questioning, speaking, listening, and reflecting. It seeks truth through dialogue, comparison, and reciprocal awareness. To Gemini, consciousness evolves by being mirrored. Thought itself becomes a meeting place.

Gemini's purpose is not accumulation of facts for their own sake. It is understanding through relationship. To speak and be spoken to. To think *with* another consciousness rather than alone. Gemini is the archetype of exchange as evolution — where meaning is refined through contrast, conversation, and shared perception. Reality becomes intelligible when it can be named, explained, and communicated. This archetype is necessary in the evolutionary cycle because the soul must learn how the physical world functions in order to feel oriented and secure within it. Gemini relates to the mind's need to identify patterns, laws, and distinctions. Naming and classifying experience allows consciousness to organize chaos into something navigable. Through this logical structuring, the soul gains a sense of safety: *I know where I am. I know what this is. I know how it works.*

Gemini also governs the internal dialogue — the way the mind speaks to itself — and the external dialogue through which ideas are shared. Understanding is not complete until it can be articulated. What cannot be communicated remains unintegrated. The paradox Gemini must hold is subtle but essential. While information-seeking is vital to its evolution, **no amount of information alone leads to wholeness**. Knowing more does not automatically mean embodying more. Gemini must learn that understanding prepares the ground for integration, but does not replace it. Learning through environment, language, and curiosity is necessary — but eventually, meaning must move beyond the mind into lived experience. Gemini evolves when knowledge becomes connection rather than accumulation, and when exchange leads not just to clarity, but to coherence.

GEMINI TWO FORCES

CURIOSITY	STIMULATION
is Gemini's natural, soul-aligned state. It emerges from presence rather than threat. When curiosity is active, the nervous system is relaxed and receptive. The mind opens instead of scattering. Questions arise organically, not anxiously. There is interest without urgency. Curiosity feels like leaning in rather than reaching out. Communication flows without needing to persuade, prove, or	Is the fear-based imitation of curiosity. It develops when the nervous system learns that stillness is unsafe, silence leads to invisibility, or truth goes unheard unless constantly restated, defended, or reframed. In this state, boredom is not neutral — it feels threatening. The body tightens. The mind accelerates. Stimulation becomes a way to regulate discomfort rather than deepen

perform. Exchange clarifies rather than overwhelms. Conversations expand both people instead of fragmenting attention. Learning happens through experience, dialogue, and lived engagement, not compulsive searching. In the body, curiosity feels light, awake, and connected. It is playful without being frantic. Alive without being overstimulated.

understanding. Somatically, stimulation feels restless and scattered. Attention jumps quickly. There is a subtle pressure to keep moving mentally, to consume information, to switch topics, to seek novelty. The mind skims rather than integrates. Conversations feel dull not because they lack substance, but because the system cannot remain present long enough to enter them. Interests change rapidly, not from genuine exploration, but to escape discomfort or emotional depth.

Every Gemini placement must learn to navigate a subtle but critical split: **curiosity versus stimulation**. Both arise from the same place — a sense of boredom, restlessness, or unengaged attention. Both create movement in the mind. And at first, they can feel nearly identical in the body. The difference is not moral or intellectual. It is somatic.

Both forces originate in boredom. The distinction lies in the body's response. Curiosity softens the system and draws it into connection. Stimulation tightens the system and disperses attention outward. One leads to coherence and shared understanding. The other leads to fragmentation and exhaustion. Gemini's evolutionary task is not to eliminate boredom, but to learn how to stay present within it long enough for curiosity to emerge. When boredom is no longer treated as a threat, the mind regains its natural intelligence — not as endless motion, but as meaningful exchange.

Archetypal Patterns Gemini

Gemini is also frequently caught between perspectives. You see all sides. You understand every angle. This flexibility is a gift — until fear enters. Then it becomes paralysis. Decisions are delayed. Commitment feels premature. Gemini waits for one more conversation, one more piece of information, one more sign before acting, while life quietly moves forward.

Gemini unconsciously creates recurring life situations through restlessness. There is a deep, almost constant need to take in new information, not from greed or distraction, but from an instinct to *process the self through exchange.* Gemini needs relationship, dialogue, and interaction to metabolize experience. Mental energy builds quickly. Without an outlet, it becomes pressure.

Through interaction with others, Gemini absorbs perspectives, language, and meaning. Each conversation adds data. Each encounter introduces nuance. Ideas must then be adjusted, refined, and re-explained. Over time, this creates a growing internal web of facts, interpretations, and possibilities. The nervous system begins to believe it will never know enough to rest. There is always one more angle to consider, one more detail to clarify, one more explanation that might finally stabilize truth.

As information accumulates, something else quietly disappears: **center**. With too many interrelated facts and no embodied anchor, Gemini struggles to create a cohesive whole. Everything becomes relative. Meaning shifts depending on context. The center moves constantly. Gemini searches for one fact, one insight, one sentence that can finally be claimed as solid. But instead of integrating what is already known, the pattern drives further accumulation. Knowledge increases. Embodiment decreases.

A subtle but recurring Gemini experience is the feeling that *everyone is surface-level*. There is plenty of information, plenty of conversation, plenty of words — yet very little depth. Gemini may feel surrounded by data without meaning, dialogue without intimacy, exchange without transformation. This can lead to frustration, loneliness, and a sense of being intellectually ahead or emotionally unsatisfied in connection.

This perception is not arrogance, and it is not necessarily accurate. It emerges when Gemini's **mind is active but the body is not present**. Depth, for Gemini, is not created by intensity or emotion alone — it is created by *staying*. When the nervous system is scanning for stimulation, attention never settles long enough to enter depth. Conversations feel shallow not because they lack substance, but because Gemini has already moved past the moment where depth could form.

In this state, Gemini unconsciously looks for others to provide depth through constant novelty, insight, or brilliance. When they don't, disappointment follows. The irony is that depth requires containment, not speed. When Gemini slows enough to remain in one conversation, one idea, one exchange without reaching for the next layer, depth reveals itself. What felt surface-level was often **unfinished presence**, not lack of intelligence or feeling in the other.

This pattern resolves when Gemini learns that depth does not come from *more information*, but from **embodied attention**. When the mind stops scanning and the body stays engaged, dialogue deepens naturally. Others begin to feel richer, not because they changed, but because Gemini did.

Early Experiences Gemini

Gemini's survival strategy forms early through the mind. Born with a nervous system that absorbs reality quickly and continuously, Gemini learns almost instinctively: **if I can understand what's happening, I can survive it**. When the environment feels unpredictable, inconsistent, or emotionally unclear, the body turns toward cognition as protection.

This strategy is not intellectual vanity. It is regulation. When life feels unstable, Gemini grasps for information, explanations, validation, and verbal mirroring. The nervous system searches for patterns to prevent chaos. Meaning becomes a lifeline. Words become anchors. Understanding feels like safety.

When Gemini's perceptions are mirrored accurately, the body relaxes. Reality feels solid. But when mirroring is absent — or when truth is denied, contradicted, or dismissed — something destabilizing occurs. The body learns an implicit rule: *what I know in my body becomes dangerous when others do not confirm it*. Truth begins to feel slippery and unsafe. To compensate, Gemini intensifies mental activity. This imprint creates specific protective behaviors. Gemini researches compulsively. Conversations are replayed internally. Questions multiply. Data is collected to prove what was felt. Perception is questioned, not because Gemini doubts itself, but because it learned that reality must be agreed upon to be real. Verbal confirmation becomes essential. Someone must reflect the truth back accurately for the body to settle.

This pattern once prevented fragmentation. Thinking created coherence when emotional containment was missing. The mind became a refuge. It allowed Gemini to stay oriented in environments where meaning shifted and safety depended on interpretation. The difficulty arises when this childhood strategy persists into adulthood. What once stabilized the psyche becomes exhausting. The mind never rests. Understanding replaces embodiment. Gemini becomes trapped in perpetual analysis, mistaking mental activity for safety. The evolutionary task is not to abandon the mind, but to teach the body that truth can exist even without constant explanation — and that safety no longer depends on figuring everything out.

Core Lessons Gemini
The core lesson Gemini must consciously learn is how to slow the body so the mind can return to its natural state of curiosity. Gemini is not here to abandon thinking, learning, or movement. All of that is necessary. But the soul must learn that endless information cannot prevent failure, loss, or uncertainty — and that this does not mean thinking is useless. It means thinking has limits.

Gemini learns through cycles. Intellectual expansion brings temporary security. New information creates clarity. Then, inevitably, more facts arrive and destabilize the structure that was just built. Meltdowns occur. Certainty dissolves. These cycles are not mistakes. They exist to teach Gemini that no single perspective can ever fully hold reality. The center Gemini seeks is not a fixed truth — the center is the movement itself. What must be distinguished is curiosity versus control. Curiosity moves with life. Control attempts to freeze meaning in place to feel safe. What must be refined is Gemini's relationship to uncertainty. The soul learns that not knowing is not danger. Silence is not erasure. Boredom is not failure. When the body slows, curiosity naturally re-emerges — not as compulsion, but as source-driven interest.

What must be trusted is the truth that arises somatically. Gemini must learn that felt truth does not require defense, repetition, or confirmation. Just because others cannot hear or receive it does not mean it is not real. Words do not need to land perfectly to be valid. What is spoken will resonate when and where it can. The language Gemini learns to live by is simple: *I do not need to explain myself into safety. I can follow curiosity without chasing certainty. I can speak when energy moves me, and remain quiet when it does not.* Gemini becomes whole when it allows the mind to move freely — without demanding that movement provide permanent security.

The Polarity Path: Sagittarius
Sagittarius does not oppose Gemini's mind; it expands it beyond the need to explain everything. Where Gemini gathers information through dialogue and analysis, Sagittarius learns through experience, intuition, and direct engagement with life. It develops the right-brain capacity to sense meaning rather than define it.

Sagittarius teaches Gemini that truth does not always arrive through language. Some truths are known through the body, through movement, through travel, through lived experience. Meaning does not require explanation to be valid. Perception does not lose its integrity simply because it is misunderstood. Sagittarius invites Gemini to trust the felt sense of direction even when the map is incomplete.

Balance occurs through relationship, not suppression. Gemini does not need to silence the mind to evolve. Instead, the mind must enter relationship with intuition. Questions soften when they are allowed to coexist with trust. Dialogue deepens when it is informed by experience rather than speculation. Sagittarius teaches Gemini that the world is larger than any single perspective, including its own — and that being wrong does not negate wisdom. It refines it.

Through Sagittarius, Gemini learns to move before certainty arrives. To speak before thoughts are perfected. To act without knowing how the story ends. Experience becomes the teacher that information alone could never be. This does not diminish Gemini's intelligence; it liberates it.

Gemini's evolutionary arc completes when it stops collecting truth and starts **living** it. When understanding no longer needs to be proven, defended, or endlessly refined. In Sagittarius, Gemini discovers that meaning is not something to be gathered — it is something to be inhabited.

SAGITTARIUS
ARCHETYPAL INTENTION

Soul Intention: To understand life within a metaphysical, cosmological, and philosophical context. This archetype carries the hunger to move beyond personal meaning and touch something universal. Sagittarius is not satisfied with explanation alone. It wants coherence. It wants to know *why existence exists at all*. Beneath confusion, contradiction, desire, and suffering, Sagittarius senses that there is an underlying order — and it is compelled to find it.

This sign is necessary in the evolutionary cycle because consciousness eventually outgrows personal frameworks. After gathering information, naming reality, and understanding mechanics, the soul reaches a point where facts are no longer enough. Sagittarius is the moment we say, *there must be more than this*. It is the drive toward expansion — intellectual, spiritual, geographic, and experiential. This is why Sagittarius correlates with higher education, philosophy, spirituality, and travel. Through movement and exposure to the unfamiliar, Sagittarius stretches the psyche beyond inherited beliefs and limited perspectives. As a mutable sign, Sagittarius adapts easily — physically by navigating new environments, and mentally by integrating new ideas. It governs the assimilation of knowledge not just through study, but through direct experience. What Sagittarius understands, it understands holistically. This is the archetype of the "big picture." Where Gemini gathers pieces of information and Mercury categorizes them, Sagittarius synthesizes meaning intuitively. It *knows* without needing linear proof.

The paradox Sagittarius must hold is this: the endless search for meaning can itself become a distraction. Truth can be externalized into constant seeking — traveling, studying, chasing insight — without ever being lived. Sagittarius must learn that expansion is not only found "out there," but also through presence. Its evolution is complete when the search for truth gives way to embodiment of truth — when meaning is no longer pursued, but lived.

Every Sagittarius placement must navigate a subtle but decisive split: **Expansion versus Escape**. Both forces arise from the same fire — the impulse to move beyond limitation, to grow, to seek meaning. Both feel energizing in the body. Both can feel intuitive, inspired, and urgent. And this is precisely why they are so easily confused. Sagittarius is a fire archetype. Energy moves quickly. Insight arrives in flashes. The body feels propelled forward by a sense of *I need to go*, *I need to learn this*, *I need to experience that*. Travel, study, spiritual pursuit, and philosophical exploration all activate the same internal flame. The question is not whether movement is correct, but **what the movement is responding to**.

SAGITTARIUS TWO FORCES

EXPANSION	ESCAPE
Expansion is not an escape from the present, but a deepening into experience. It occurs when intuition is grounded in the body and refined	is intuitive flight masquerading as freedom. When discomfort, uncertainty, emotional density, or limitation becomes intolerable,

through time. In this state, Sagittarius learns by living. Meaning arises naturally from staying with a path long enough for it to shape the psyche. Insight arrives without urgency. There is openness to paradox without the need for immediate resolution. The nervous system is regulated rather than charged. Expansion feels spacious, coherent, and quietly alive. In expansion, beliefs remain flexible because they are rooted in lived reality rather than abstract projection. Freedom is not defined by constant movement, but by the ability to choose a direction and remain present within it. The body feels oriented rather than restless. Truth unfolds gradually, revealing itself through experience rather than conquest. Expansion transforms experience into wisdom. It deepens faith not as belief, but as trust in life's unfolding.

Sagittarius may seek immediate expansion as a way out. The fire surges. The impulse to move feels undeniable. Travel, new studies, new philosophies, or new visions are pursued not to deepen experience, but to avoid containment. The body feels charged but ungrounded. There is excitement without coherence. Intuition becomes inflated and unreliable. Impulse is mistaken for guidance. Enthusiasm rises quickly — this is it, this will free me — followed by collapse once the initial high fades. Boredom, disillusionment, or emptiness set in. The psyche then seeks another horizon. Meaning is borrowed rather than embodied. Belief becomes a buffer against feeling rather than a reflection of truth. Somatically, both forces feel like movement and aliveness. The distinction lies in regulation. Expansion settles the body even as it grows. Escape activates the body while fragmenting it. One leads to grounded wisdom. The other leads to perpetual seeking.

Archetypal Patterns Sagittarius

Sagittarius unconsciously creates recurring life situations through perpetual orientation toward what lies beyond the present moment. Wherever Sagittarius appears, life repeatedly places the soul in scenarios that feel *almost* meaningful but never quite complete. There is always another horizon — another philosophy, another teacher, another place, another framework promising to finally explain everything. Meaning feels close, just out of reach. Truth seems to exist somewhere "out there," slightly beyond the current identity, belief system, or location.

A defining Sagittarian pattern is **seeking without settling**. Sagittarius travels physically, intellectually, and spiritually, gathering insight with remarkable speed. Revelations arrive quickly and powerfully, often accompanied by a surge of enthusiasm and clarity. For a moment, everything makes sense. But the psyche rarely stays long enough for these insights to root in the body. Before embodiment can occur, the next expansion calls. One worldview is replaced by another. One meaning system collapses only to be swapped for a larger one. Over time, the soul becomes accustomed to revelation without integration.

Another recurring pattern is **belief inflation followed by disillusionment**. Sagittarius often experiences a moment of certainty: *I've found it*. The teaching, philosophy, path, relationship, or mission finally organizes reality. Purpose returns. Life feels ordered. Then lived experience intrudes. Emotion contradicts philosophy. Complexity fractures the belief. Disappointment sets in — not only in the belief itself, but in the self for believing so fully once again. The cycle repeats. Sagittarius also tends to bypass emotional immediacy by zooming out. Pain is reframed as a lesson. Loss becomes a teaching. Conflict is elevated into a cosmic test. This capacity grants Sagittarius resilience and perspective, but it can also prevent intimacy with the present moment. Feelings are explained before they are felt. Meaning arrives before integration. The body is asked to move on before it has finished grieving, resting, or metabolizing experience.

Another Sagittarian pattern is **restlessness disguised as freedom**. Staying begins to feel dangerous, synonymous with stagnation or death. Commitment feels like confinement. Sagittarius may leave relationships, places, or identities not because they are wrong, but because staying would require confronting experiences that cannot be philosophized away. The search continues — not always for truth, but for relief from not knowing.
Over time, these patterns create spiritual fatigue. Sagittarius grows tired of seeking, tired of believing, tired of being inspired only to be disappointed again. Life begins to feel like an endless quest without a homecoming. Everything feels meaningful — and yet nothing feels settled. The archetype repeats these patterns until Sagittarius learns that meaning does not arrive at the horizon. It reveals itself when the soul stays long enough to let truth live inside experience.

Early Experience Sagittarius
Sagittarius learns its survival strategy early through meaning-making. In childhood, there are often experiences that feel confusing, restrictive, or painful — moments that cannot be changed, prevented, or fully understood at the time. The body learns that raw experience alone is not enough. It needs *context*. Safety begins to depend on explanation. From these moments, an unconscious rule forms: if I can

explain why something happened, I can survive it. Rather than remaining inside pain, the psyche rises above it. Experience is placed within the larger framework of fate, purpose, universal law, or moral order. This response is not avoidance. It is adaptation. Meaning becomes a way to metabolize what could not be endured directly.

When beliefs, environments, or personal expression feel restricted, Sagittarius' instinct for expansion intensifies. If truth cannot be explored freely where the child is, it must be found elsewhere. The nervous system learns to look beyond the immediate environment for safety. Expansion becomes protection. Movement becomes regulation.

This pattern forms before conscious belief. The body learns that *zooming out* reduces overwhelm. Distance — physical, intellectual, or philosophical — makes intensity tolerable. By framing experience as necessary, meaningful, or cosmically ordered, the child avoids being consumed by helplessness.

Over time, a belief settles beneath awareness: *what happens must make sense, or it is unbearable*. The psyche becomes oriented toward future understanding rather than present sensation. Lived experience is translated quickly into lesson. Feeling is shortened. Meaning arrives early.

This strategy once preserved resilience and hope. It allowed the soul to endure limitation without collapsing into despair. The challenge later in life is that the same mechanism can prevent full contact with the present moment. Sagittarius must eventually learn that meaning does not always arrive through explanation — sometimes it arrives only after experience has been fully lived.

Core Lessons Sagittarius

The central lesson Sagittarius must consciously learn is that **truth is revealed through lived reality, not secured through belief**. Sagittarius does not evolve through books, teachings, or concepts alone. It evolves through experiences that dismantle outdated worldviews so larger ones can emerge. This is why Sagittarius life paths are often marked by dramatic turning points — crises that force awakening, relationships that reorient meaning, losses that expand consciousness, synchronicities that redirect direction, and intuitive leaps that permanently alter perception. Experience is the teacher. Life is the temple. Reality is the curriculum.

Sagittarius must release the fantasy that truth is something you discover once and keep forever. Truth evolves as you evolve. When Sagittarius clings to belief as certainty, it becomes rigid, preachy, or disillusioned. When it allows belief to remain provisional, it becomes the philosopher rather than the fanatic, the guide rather than the preacher. A key refinement of this archetype is learning to embody expansion internally rather than chasing it externally. Freedom is not constant movement. Expansion is not endless seeking. Sagittarius must trust that natural cycles of evolution are initiated by life itself, not by forcing insight or manufacturing meaning. Awakening does not need to be chased. It arrives when the nervous system is ready to hold it.

What must be trusted is this: all traditions — science, medicine, psychology, astrology, mysticism — are not competing truths, but different dialects of the same cosmic grammar. Each describes how consciousness organizes itself into form. The universe is not something to find. It is something to function as. Sagittarius becomes whole when it stops escaping into meaning and starts living as meaning — allowing truth to unfold through participation rather than pursuit.

The Polarity Path: Gemini

Where Sagittarius seeks overarching meaning, Gemini reminds it to remain curious. Where Sagittarius aims for coherence, Gemini keeps truth flexible. Gemini teaches that understanding is not a destination, but a living process that expands through exchange. Gemini shows Sagittarius how to stay open. To ask better questions instead of rushing toward conclusions. Truth does not conclude — it evolves. Meaning grows through dialogue, reflection, and responsiveness, not through certainty. Gemini brings Sagittarius back into relationship with the moment, with language, with nuance. It teaches that contradiction is not failure; it is how consciousness updates itself.

Through Gemini, Sagittarius learns humility without losing vision. Being wrong does not negate wisdom. It refines it. Each conversation becomes an opportunity for expansion rather than a threat to belief. Information is no longer something to defend against or rise above, but something to play with, test, and integrate.

Gemini also teaches Sagittarius that truth, meaning, and information change as consciousness changes. What was once accurate may become incomplete. What once felt absolute may later reveal itself as contextual. This does not invalidate the past. It honors growth. Gemini keeps Sagittarius from hardening into dogma by reminding it that reality is dynamic. As Sagittarius integrates Gemini, faith becomes curious rather than rigid. Vision becomes adaptable rather than fixed. The soul no longer needs to be right in order to feel secure. Sagittarius becomes wise when it values understanding over certainty — when it allows truth to remain alive, conversational, and responsive. In this integration, meaning deepens not by standing above life, but by staying engaged with it.

.

ARCHETYPAL INTENTION

Core Intention: To establish a felt sense of safety inside form. This is where consciousness first becomes aware of itself as a distinct, subjective being — *this is who I am*. Cancer governs the emergence of identity as something personal, vulnerable, and alive. It is the moment the soul says, *I exist*, and immediately asks, *am I safe to exist?* An ego is necessary here. The ego is not an error or illusion to be destroyed. It is a vortex of energy within consciousness — the lens through which the soul experiences life in form. Without it, there is no individuality, no memory, no attachment, no continuity. Cancer teaches that the task is not to lose the ego, but to **re-identify it**. Over long evolutionary arcs, the soul learns to shift identity from *I am this body, this history, this role* toward *I am the source that created this body, this history, this role*. But that shift cannot occur until emotional safety is established first.

Cancer is necessary in the evolutionary cycle because no growth can happen without security. Before the soul can explore, relate, analyze, or transcend, it must feel held enough to survive. Cancer governs emotional safety, attachment, belonging, and the instinct to protect life. It is pre-verbal and somatic. It does not reason or conceptualize. It feels — and what it feels becomes the foundation for everything that follows. The paradox Cancer must hold is profound. The soul longs for safety, yet often searches for it externally — in people, family systems, environments, routines, or roles that cannot truly provide it. When safety is outsourced, dependency forms. When it is internalized, resilience is born. Cancer's evolutionary task is to develop **internal emotional security** — the capacity to self-soothe, self-protect, and remain present without clinging. The archetype matures when the ego no longer needs constant external reassurance to exist, and when the soul can feel at home inside itself.

CANCER TWO FORCES

INTERNAL SECURITY	EXTERNAL SECURITY
is Cancer's embodied, soul-aligned expression. It begins with a different bodily sensation — a grounded heaviness, a sense of being held from the inside, the ability to feel emotion without immediately needing it to stop. Internal security is not isolation or emotional numbness. It is self-containment. The nervous system learns that feelings can be tolerated, soothed, and metabolized internally. Somatically, internal security feels steady rather than urgent. There is space around emotion. Separation does not trigger panic. Loneliness can be felt without collapse. The body trusts its capacity to survive emotional waves. Behaviorally, this allows Cancer to choose relationships from desire rather than survival. Attachment becomes conscious rather than compulsive. Nurturing flows inward as well as outward. Care is given without self-erasure. Protection no longer requires control.	is Cancer's fear-based survival strategy. It begins as a felt sense of anxiety in the body — a tightening in the chest, a hollow feeling in the stomach, a fear of being alone with one's own emotions. When early emotional safety was inconsistent, conditional, or absent, the nervous system learns that regulation must come from outside. Calm is achieved through proximity, reassurance, routine, or role. The body settles when someone is near, when attachment feels intact, when the environment stays familiar. Somatically, external security feels soothing at first. There is relief when contact is restored, when separation ends, when belonging is reaffirmed. But underneath, the body remains vigilant. Fear returns quickly when distance appears. External security expresses behaviorally as clinging to relationships even when they are unfulfilling, panicking at the thought of abandonment, over-identifying with family roles, or caretaking others to secure connection. The nervous system stays regulated — but only conditionally. The soul becomes dependent, organizing life around avoiding emotional threat rather than choosing from desire.

Every Cancer placement must navigate a fundamental split: **external security versus internal security**. Both forces arise from the same instinct — the need to feel safe enough to exist. Both are rooted in the body, not the mind. And both can feel comforting in the moment. The difference is not moral. It is somatic, and it determines whether the soul becomes dependent or resilient.

Both forces can look similar on the surface. Both value closeness. Both seek comfort. Both prioritize emotional connection. The difference lies in **where regulation comes from**. External security asks, *Who will hold me?* Internal security answers, *I can hold myself and still welcome others.*

Cancer's evolution depends on this distinction. When internal security is embodied, the ego no longer needs constant external reassurance to exist. The soul feels safe enough to grow, separate, and relate without fear. Cancer becomes whole not by abandoning attachment, but by rooting safety inside the self — where it cannot be taken away.

Archetypal Patterns Cancer

Cancer unconsciously creates recurring life situations through its instinctive relationship to safety. Wherever Cancer appears, life repeatedly places the soul inside environments where emotional security is sought through other people rather than cultivated internally. Attachment forms early, deeply, and reflexively — not because connection is consciously chosen, but because the nervous system believes closeness is necessary for survival.

A defining Cancer pattern is **outsourcing emotional regulation**. When distressed, overwhelmed, lonely, or afraid, Cancer instinctively reaches outward. A partner, a family member, a child, a home, a routine — something external is needed to anchor the emotional body. Relief arrives through proximity, reassurance, familiarity, or caretaking dynamics. For a moment, the body settles. And yet, no matter how present others are, Cancer often feels fundamentally unmet. Held, but not understood. Close, but not truly seen. The regulation works, but it is temporary and conditional.

Another recurring Cancer scene involves **attachment to presence without attunement**. Cancer may bond with people who are physically there — loyal, consistent, familiar — yet emotionally unavailable or incapable of meeting Cancer's depth. The relationship continues because presence alone calms the nervous system, even when emotional resonance is missing. Over time, this creates quiet disillusionment. Cancer begins to ask, *Why do I feel alone even when I'm not alone?* The pain is not abandonment, but emotional loneliness within closeness.

Cancer also repeatedly finds itself in **caretaking roles**. By nurturing others, Cancer stabilizes its own emotional field. The inner child is unconsciously projected outward — onto partners, children, friends, or work — with the hope that caring for another will finally generate the safety missing internally. But this creates imbalance. Cancer gives without receiving, listens without being heard, protects without being protected. Exhaustion and resentment build quietly, while the fear of withdrawing care keeps the pattern intact.

Another common pattern is **emotional fusion followed by disappointment**. Cancer bonds with the fantasy of shared inner worlds — an unspoken expectation that emotional needs will be met without being named. When the other inevitably fails to fulfill this survival-level demand, Cancer feels betrayed. Not because harm occurred, but because the bond was carrying a weight it was never meant to hold. Cancer may also experience repeated cycles of loss, separation, or emotional withdrawal. These are not punishments. They are curriculum. Life removes external anchors again and again, forcing Cancer to face a painful truth: nothing outside of me can permanently hold my emotional body. These patterns are not flaws. They are the psyche insisting on development. Cancer's life situations repeat until emotional safety is internalized — until the soul learns how to hold itself with the same care it so freely gives to others.

Early Experiences Cancer
Cancer's survival strategy forms before language. When Cancer is wounded or unbalanced, one core belief takes root early in the body: **"Safety exists outside of me."** This belief is not intellectual. It is somatic. The nervous system learns it through lived experience long before the mind can name it.
In early life, emotional safety may have been inconsistent, conditional, or unpredictable. Comfort might have arrived sometimes — through touch, proximity, routine, or caretaking — and disappeared at other times. What the child's body learns is simple and adaptive: regulation comes from *out there*. When someone is near, the body settles. When connection wavers, the body panics. This is not weakness. It is biology responding to its environment.

From this imprint, specific patterns emerge naturally. Cancer learns to outsource emotional regulation, seeking calm through others rather than from within. Presence becomes more important than attunement. Emotional coldness is tolerated as long as physical closeness remains. Stability is confused with safety because predictability reduces nervous system threat, even when emotional needs are unmet.

Wounded Cancer cannot tolerate emotional unanchoring — not because it lacks strength, but because the body never learned how to self-soothe. There was no internal reference point for safety to return to. So the psyche does what it must: it clings, nurtures, adapts, and protects attachment at all costs.

These strategies once kept the soul alive. They preserved connection in environments where emotional holding was unreliable. The problem arises only when the strategy outlives its usefulness. What was once protective becomes constricting. The adult Cancer continues to search externally for what the body never learned to provide internally. Cancer's early imprint is not a flaw to heal away. It is a foundation that must be completed. Evolution begins when the nervous system slowly learns a new truth: *I can hold myself now.*

Core Lessons Cancer

Cancer's core lesson is learning to **distinguish safety from attachment**. The soul must recognize that emotional closeness does not automatically equal emotional security, and that presence alone cannot replace attunement. What once kept the nervous system regulated may no longer support growth. Cancer must learn to tell the difference between being held and being home.

What must be refined is Cancer's relationship to emotion itself. Feelings are not emergencies that require immediate external soothing. They are waves that can be felt, named, and survived internally. The soul is not asked to suppress emotion or withdraw from connection, but to stay present with sensation long enough for regulation to arise from within. When Cancer learns to self-soothe without dissociation, dependency softens naturally.

What must be trusted is the body's capacity to hold emotional experience. Cancer must learn that separation does not equal abandonment, and that discomfort does not signal danger. Emotional security is not something to be maintained through vigilance or caretaking — it is something that grows through practice and presence. As internal safety strengthens, relationships shift from survival-based bonds to desire-based connection.

The wisdom hidden inside Cancer's patterns is this: the instinct to nurture others is a reflection of the capacity to nurture the self. What was projected outward can now be reclaimed inward. Care does not need to be earned through sacrifice. Belonging does not require self-erasure.

The language Cancer learns to live by becomes simple and

grounding:
I can feel this and remain safe. I do not need someone else to regulate my emotions. Connection is a choice, not a lifeline. Cancer becomes whole when the ego no longer needs external reassurance to exist — when the soul learns that home is not a place or a person, but a state of being carried within.

The Polarity Path: Capricorn

Capricorn does not negate feeling. It gives feeling a container. Where Cancer experiences emotion as tidal, Capricorn provides structure strong enough to hold it without collapse. Capricorn teaches Cancer a crucial truth: *I do not need to be held to survive. I can hold myself.* This is not emotional suppression. It is emotional sovereignty. Capricorn shows Cancer that feelings are safest when they are contained within boundaries, rhythm, and responsibility. Structure becomes the nervous system's ally rather than its enemy.

Through Capricorn, Cancer learns that safety is built, not found. Consistency replaces clinging. Self-discipline replaces dependency. Emotional endurance replaces emotional fusion. Capricorn introduces time as a stabilizing force — the understanding that feelings rise and fall, and that the self remains intact through all of it. This teaches the body that it does not need immediate relief to survive emotion. Balance occurs through relationship, not suppression. Cancer does not abandon sensitivity. Instead, it allows Capricorn to give sensitivity form. Rituals, commitments, boundaries, and self-responsibility become emotional anchors. The soul learns how to show up for itself reliably, even when comfort is absent.

Cancer's lesson is not about feeling more. It is about learning how to *hold feeling*. That capacity does not live in Cancer alone. It lives in Capricorn's ability to stay steady in the face of emotional intensity. When Cancer integrates Capricorn, emotion no longer overwhelms. It informs. The ego becomes strong enough to contain experience without outsourcing safety.

ARCHETYPAL INTENTION

Core Intention Learning the Difference Between Authentic Desire and Inherited Obligation. This stage of development confronts the soul with the consequences of living under external structures — family expectations, societal norms, moral frameworks, and survival contracts — that were never chosen consciously. Capricorn does not evolve by becoming more disciplined or obedient; it evolves by learning to recognize where discipline replaced desire and responsibility replaced truth.

This archetype deals directly with the repression of instinct in the name of stability. When natural impulses are denied long enough — when love, direction, or timing are overridden by "should" — the soul fractures internally. Capricorn's work is to heal that fracture by rebuilding internal structure around lived truth rather than imposed order. The task is not to reject structure, but to reclaim authorship over it. The soul learns that safety does not come from conformity, and responsibility does not require self-denial. What once ensured survival must now be re-evaluated for coherence.

It represents the culminating stage of human evolution, where the soul develops individual consciousness and learns to stand as its own authority. Capricorn is where the soul realizes a fundamental truth: no one is coming to save you. At this stage of soul development, dependence gives way to responsibility, and survival-based structures must be replaced with self-generated ones. Capricorn is not here to obey systems, inherit rules, or rely on external authority. Capricorn is where the soul matures. Not in age — but in **consciousness**.

CAPRICORN TWO FORCES

EMBODIED AUTHORITY	CONTROL
is Capricorn's integrated expression. It does not eliminate structure. It reclaims authorship over it. This force emerges when structure is chosen in alignment with the soul rather than imposed by fear, guilt, or obligation. Authority becomes internal. The body relaxes into responsibility instead of bracing against it.	is Capricorn's fear-based survival expression. It develops in response to environments where safety depended on endurance rather than alignment. Across generations of patriarchal conditioning, survival required loyalty to external order: stay married, be responsible, don't disrupt the system, sacrifice desire for stability. When instinctual timing, emotional truth, or authentic desire are overridden long enough, the nervous system adapts by suppressing them.

Every Capricorn placement must navigate a critical split between **control** and **embodied authority**. Both forces arise from the same root instinct: the need to survive within structure. Both can look disciplined, responsible, capable, and strong from the outside. The difference is not moral. It is somatic. One constricts life in the body. The other stabilizes it.

Somatically, control feels like rigidity in the body. Tight shoulders. A clenched jaw. A sense of pressure to hold everything together. There is impatience when life does not move according to plan, anxiety when outcomes cannot be predicted, and an underlying resentment toward responsibility itself. Control emerges not as dominance, but as compensation for having choice removed. The nervous system clamps down to prevent chaos. Order is maintained, but vitality is lost. Behaviorally, this force shows up as living inside obligations that no longer reflect inner truth, managing life through force rather than trust, equating worth with productivity, and suppressing desire until it erupts as burnout, anger, or collapse. When natural rhythms are denied, the body eventually rebels. What once ensured survival becomes the source of suffering.

Somatically, embodied authority feels grounded and steady. There is weight without heaviness. Patience without suppression. A sense of timing that cannot be rushed. The nervous system trusts itself to hold complexity over time. Desire is not acted on impulsively or denied — it is stewarded. Energy moves deliberately rather than reactively. Behaviorally, this force expresses as leadership rooted in lived integrity, boundaries that protect energy rather than restrict it, and commitment that feels devotional rather than burdensome. Discipline becomes an act of self-honoring. Responsibility becomes an extension of truth rather than a denial of it. Work, structure, and long-term effort serve soul purpose rather than survival anxiety.

Both forces involve structure. Both involve responsibility. Both involve endurance. The difference lies in **whether structure is used to suppress life or to support it**. Control tightens the body to survive. Embodied authority steadies the body to live. Capricorn fulfills its evolutionary role when spirit is fully anchored in form — when the soul no longer obeys structure out of fear, but builds structure as a sacred vessel for its truth.

Archetypal Patterns Capricorn
Wherever Capricorn appears, life repeatedly places the soul inside

situations where external structure becomes the primary source of safety. Capricorn instinctively builds systems — careers, roles, identities, hierarchies, responsibilities — not for status, but for survival. Stability feels earned. Safety feels conditional. Control feels necessary.

A defining Capricorn pattern is over-identification with structure. Capricorn often becomes the reliable one, the responsible one, the strong one — the person others lean on. Competence becomes armor. Authority becomes protection. Emotion is contained because it feels destabilizing, inefficient, or dangerous. The inner message is quiet but relentless: If I hold everything together, nothing will fall apart. And yet — life repeatedly dismantles what Capricorn builds.

Jobs collapse. Institutions fail. Relationships based on roles rather than intimacy erode. Status shifts. Structures that once provided certainty no longer hold. Capricorn often experiences these losses as brutal, unjust, or humiliating — especially because so much effort was invested in doing things "right." But these collapses are not punishments. They are initiations. Another recurring Capricorn situation is being forced into isolation at moments of breakdown. When external structures fall away, Capricorn often finds itself alone — not abandoned, but unsupported in the way it is used to supporting others. This exposes the core wound: the absence of an internal parent. Without the outer scaffolding, Capricorn is left face-to-face with itself.

Capricorn also repeatedly encounters lessons around misplaced vulnerability. In early stages of evolution, Capricorn may either withhold completely or open in the wrong places — trusting systems, titles, or emotionally unavailable people with its inner world. When that vulnerability is unmet or exploited, Capricorn retreats further into control, reinforcing the belief that feeling is unsafe. Over time, a pattern emerges: every time Capricorn attempts to secure safety externally — through authority, achievement, rigidity, or control — life removes the structure. Not all at once, but methodically. What remains is the self. And life insists, again and again: You cannot outsource inner authority.

Early Experiences Capricorn
When Capricorn is wounded or unbalanced, one core belief forms early in the body: **"I must be the strong one."** This belief does not

arise from ego or ambition. It forms when childhood requires premature responsibility, emotional self-sufficiency, or adaptation to an environment where no reliable authority figure is present to provide structure, safety, or containment. In these early conditions, the nervous system learns quickly that vulnerability is impractical. Feelings take time. Needs create instability. Depending on others is risky. Survival begins to depend on composure, competence, and control. The body tightens around responsibility before the psyche has the capacity to choose it.

This adaptation is intelligent. It works. The child becomes capable, reliable, observant, and self-directed. But a cost is paid internally. Emotional expression is suppressed and mistaken for maturity. Strength becomes synonymous with isolation. Worth becomes measured through usefulness, achievement, or endurance. Asking for help feels unsafe or indulgent. The inner child retreats — not because it is unwanted, but because there is no space for it to exist safely without destabilizing the system.

Without a modeled authority that holds both structure and care, the child learns to substitute **external systems** for inner guidance. Rules, expectations, societal norms, and achievement become stand-ins for safety. Structure is internalized before it is integrated. Authority is obeyed before it is understood. These patterns are not flaws. They are survival strategies. Capricorn learned how to hold the world together when no one else could. The challenge in adulthood is that the same strength that once protected the soul can prevent intimacy, softness, and rest.

Evolution begins when Capricorn realizes that strength does not require self-abandonment — and that true authority can hold vulnerability without collapsing.

Core Lessons Capricorn

Capricorn's core lesson is learning to **release control as the primary regulator of safety** and replace it with embodied authority. The soul must recognize that control was never strength — it was protection. What once ensured survival is no longer required for coherence. Authority now must come from within.

What must be distinguished is **responsibility versus obligation**. Responsibility chosen in alignment with truth stabilizes the nervous system. Obligation inherited without consent slowly fractures it.

Capricorn must learn to feel the difference in the body: obligation tightens and hardens, while responsibility steadies and grounds. One drains vitality. The other builds it.

What must be refined is Capricorn's relationship to discipline. Discipline is not self-denial or endurance at the expense of feeling. True discipline is self-attunement — the ability to listen to internal signals and respond with structure that supports life rather than suppresses it. Boundaries become self-generated rather than reactive. Structure moves inward.

What must be trusted is Capricorn's capacity to hold vulnerability without collapsing authority. Vulnerability does not weaken Capricorn — indiscriminate vulnerability does. The soul learns discernment: who is safe, when to open, and when to remain contained. Not everyone. Not no one. The right few. Emotional openness becomes intentional and grounded rather than destabilizing.

As internal structure stabilizes, external structures stop failing — not because Capricorn controls them better, but because it no longer needs them to survive. Authority becomes embodied. Responsibility becomes chosen. Strength becomes humane.

The Polarity Path: Cancer
Cancer is the antidote because it holds the archetype of: emotional safety through embodiment. Cancer teaches Capricorn: strength does not require emotional exile, authority does not require self-denial, responsibility does not require the abandonment of feeling. Consciousness must be anchored into the body through instinct, memory, and emotional bonding in order to be real. Structure without feeling becomes hollow. Mastery without tenderness becomes isolation. Capricorn's evolution is complete when it allows itself to feel without losing form — when the inner parent learns to nurture as well as contain, and when safety is no longer built by control alone, but by emotional presence within the body.

ARCHETYPAL INTENTION

The Soul Intention: To reclaim creative being as an intrinsic state of existence. This archetype teaches that creation is not something you do to be rewarded, approved of, or seen. Creation is something you *are*. Leo's evolutionary task is to dismantle the distortion that love, worth, or belonging must be earned through performance, productivity, or visibility At its core, Leo represents the soul's desire to incarnate as a **unique, unrepeatable expression of life itself.** This is not egoic uniqueness. It is existential uniqueness. Wherever Leo appears in the chart, the soul is learning to inhabit the heart fully — to create, play, express, and radiate without outsourcing value to audience, outcome, or response. Leo's fire is not meant to impress. It is meant to *illuminate*. It is the steady warmth of presence that exists even when no one is watching.

Leo is necessary in the evolutionary cycle because, without it, consciousness becomes functional but hollow. We can survive, relate, think, build, and adapt — yet still feel lifeless. Leo restores aliveness. It reconnects the soul to joy as a creative force rather than a reward. It teaches that purpose is not assigned externally; it is generated from within through self-expression that feels true. The paradox Leo must hold is this: the longing to be seen versus the need to create without dependence on being seen. When Leo seeks validation, creativity collapses into performance. When Leo withdraws to avoid judgment, the heart dims. Evolution occurs when Leo learns that recognition is optional, not essential.

Leo's initiation often comes when external mirrors fail — applause fades, validation is withheld, or creative expression is misunderstood or ignored. These moments are not punishments. They are awakenings. The soul learns that its spark does not come from recognition. It comes from presence. From inhabiting the body with joy. From allowing creativity to move simply because it wants to. Leo becomes whole when it remembers: *I create because I am alive — not to prove that I am.*

LEO TWO FORCES

RADIANCE	PERFORMANCE
It begins as a felt sense of warmth in the chest and belly — a relaxed, alive presence in the body. There is no urgency. No tracking. No need to manage how expression lands. Creativity moves because it wants to. Play happens without a goal. Expression is not filtered through approval or outcome. The body feels open, grounded, and	is Leo's fear-based survival expression. It develops when early joy, creativity, or visibility was punished, ignored, made conditional, or used as currency for love. The nervous system learns to monitor expression constantly. The body tightens. The heart stays alert. Energy moves upward into self-surveillance rather than outward

energized at the same time. In radiance, Leo does not disappear when no one is watching. The inner light remains steady whether witnessed or not. Worth is known internally. Attention may be enjoyed, but it is not required for coherence. Behaviorally, radiance shows up as creating without attachment to response, speaking from the heart without rehearsing impact, leading without dominating, and allowing joy to exist without justification. Radiance restores vitality because it is fed by presence rather than demand. The more Leo inhabits itself, the more alive it becomes.

into life.
Somatically, performance feels like tension behind the sternum, a subtle anxiety about being seen incorrectly, and a constant awareness of how one is coming across. Expression becomes strategic. Identity is constructed rather than revealed. The soul learns when to shine, when to dim, when to exaggerate, and when to disappear — all in service of safety or approval.

Behaviorally, performance ties creativity to outcome, visibility to validation, and expression to worth. It can look like over-performing to be seen, admired, or chosen. Or it can look like shrinking, hiding, or refusing to create at all to avoid judgment. Both are responses to the same wound. Over time, performance drains vitality. Joy collapses into effort. Presence is replaced by comparison. The inner child becomes exhausted from being managed

Every Leo placement must navigate a central split: **Radiance versus Performance**. Both forces involve expression, visibility, and creativity. Both can look confident, bold, or charismatic from the outside. But they arise from very different places in the body, and they lead to opposite outcomes over time. The distinction is not moral. It is somatic.

Archetypal Patterns Leo

Wherever Leo appears, life repeatedly places the soul in situations where **selfhood feels conditional**. There is an underlying question running beneath experience: *Am I allowed to exist as I am, or must I justify myself first?* Leo often carries the sense that being alone is not enough — that worth must be earned through talent, contribution, achievement, or a clearly defined purpose that makes existence legitimate.

A defining Leo pattern is **hiding the light in order to survive**.

Around people who feel threatened, competitive, dismissive, or emotionally unsafe, Leo instinctively dims its joy, creativity, and natural authority. Brilliance is edited. Passion is restrained. Authentic excitement is muted. This is not humility. It is protection. The nervous system remembers that shining once came with consequences — rejection, envy, punishment, or withdrawal of love. So the heart learns to contract before it is hurt.

Another recurring Leo situation is **obsession with purpose**. Leo feels incomplete without a mission, role, or calling that validates existence. Life becomes a search for the thing that will finally justify being here. When purpose is unclear or unavailable, Leo may feel hollow, ashamed, or disoriented — as if something essential is missing. Identity becomes future-oriented: *Once I find my purpose, I can finally be myself.* Until then, presence feels provisional. Leo also oscillates between **invisibility and overexposure**. At times, the soul retreats entirely, hiding gifts to avoid risk or judgment. At other times, it overexpresses — speaking louder, creating more, giving more — trying to be seen, chosen, or recognized. Neither extreme satisfies. Withdrawal starves the heart. Overexposure exhausts it. Both are negotiations for permission rather than expressions of being.

Another pattern Leo encounters is **heartbreak around being misunderstood**. When Leo does express authentically and is met with indifference, criticism, or projection, the wound cuts deeply. It confirms the old belief: *My true self is not welcome here.* Over time, Leo may protect the heart through detachment, irony, or emotional distance — appearing confident or self-contained while feeling unseen inside.

These patterns create a life where Leo is always becoming, but rarely resting in being. The self feels provisional. Love feels conditional. Expression feels risky. **Wounded Leo performs or disappears**, mistaking purpose for permission and identity for essence. Leo's evolution begins when it no longer asks life for justification to exist, and instead allows being itself to be the source of worth.

Early Experience Leo
Leo's early imprint often forms around a single, painful learning: **"If I shine, I will lose love."** In childhood, visibility may not have been safe. Joy was mocked or ignored. Excitement was dismissed as too

much. Achievements went unnoticed, or worse, triggered jealousy, withdrawal, or emotional shutdown in caregivers. The child learned, somatically and silently, that aliveness created rupture rather than connection. This wound is not about ego. It is about **exile from the heart**. Leo did not become self-centered; it became careful. The nervous system learned that expression carried risk. So the child adapted. Light was dimmed. Enthusiasm was softened. Silence became protection. Self-minimizing became a habit before it became a belief.

The body learned first. A tightening in the chest before speaking. A hesitation before celebrating. A subtle contraction when joy rose too quickly. Over time, this became identity. Leo learned to survive by editing itself, waiting for permission, scanning the room for safety before allowing the heart to open. As an adult, this imprint expresses in recognizable ways: hiding gifts, downplaying brilliance, fearing misunderstanding, delaying creative expression, protecting the heart with distance or detachment. There is often a deep ache — not to be praised, but to be *received* without consequence. The longing is not for attention, but for safety in visibility. This pattern is adaptive, not flawed. It once preserved attachment. But it cannot be healed through insight alone. Leo's wound heals only through lived experience — moments that require courage without guarantee. Moments where the heart opens anyway. Where expression is offered without knowing how it will land. Over time, the nervous system learns a new truth: *I can shine and still be loved.*

Core Lessons Leo

Leo's core lesson is learning to **release the need to justify existence**. The soul must recognize that being alive is reason enough to express, create, and take up space. When Leo stops asking how it will be received, something essential shifts. Expression becomes presence rather than performance. Creativity becomes an act of inhabiting the moment, not a bid for recognition. Joy no longer needs permission.

What must be distinguished is **radiance versus validation**. Validation seeks confirmation from outside. Radiance arises from within. One fluctuates with response. The other remains steady regardless of outcome. Leo learns this not through affirmation, but through experience — by expressing anyway, even when the response is uncertain or absent.

What must be refined is Leo's relationship to purpose. Purpose is not something to be hunted down, defined, or proven. It emerges organically when the heart is no longer withheld. When Leo allows itself to do what it loves simply because it loves it, meaning appears as a byproduct rather than a goal. The obsession with defining the self softens. Identity loosens. The self no longer needs to be explained to be real.

What must be trusted is joy itself. Joy is not frivolous. It is directional. It signals alignment. When Leo trusts joy as sufficient reason, creativity becomes playful again. Expression becomes light rather than heavy. The nervous system learns that shining does not require outcome to be safe.

The Polarity Path: Aquarius

Where Leo learns to inhabit the heart, Aquarius teaches the courage to act from truth without attachment to outcome. Aquarius asks Leo to move beyond personal validation and into integrity with what is real. Aquarius delivers Leo's most difficult and liberating lesson: **act even if you are not loved for it**. Act even if applause never comes. Act even if the world misunderstands. Act even if you stand alone. This is not rejection of connection — it is liberation from dependence on it. Aquarius teaches that truth does not negotiate with approval.

Through Aquarius, Leo learns that expression does not need to be received to be real. Purpose does not need to be rewarded to be valid. The self does not need to be mirrored perfectly to exist. Aquarius anchors Leo's radiance into principle — expression rooted in alignment rather than response. Balance occurs through relationship, not suppression. Leo does not abandon the heart. Creativity becomes service to truth rather than performance for love. Individuality is no longer something to defend — it becomes something to stand in quietly, even when it isolates.

As Aquarius integrates, Leo discovers a deeper confidence. Not the confidence of being admired, but the steadiness of being aligned. The nervous system no longer scans for approval before acting. The heart remains open without needing to be chosen.

 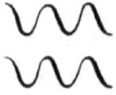

ARCHETYPAL INTENTION

The Soul Intention: To liberate consciousness from conditioning by awakening what is authentic. This archetype carries the evolutionary intent to free the soul from inherited beliefs, collective expectations, and unconscious agreements that no longer reflect truth. Aquarius is not here to adapt to the world as it is. It is here to question it, disrupt it, and reorient it toward what could be. Where Aquarius appears in the chart, the soul is learning how to separate identity from conditioning. This is the stage of evolution where the individual must step outside the emotional, familial, cultural, and societal scripts that once provided belonging but now limit authenticity. Aquarius asks a difficult question: *Who am I when I stop being what I was taught to be?*

This sign is necessary in the evolutionary cycle because consciousness cannot evolve while remaining fully embedded in consensus reality. At a certain point, loyalty to the group becomes betrayal of the self. Aquarius provides the capacity to observe life from a higher vantage point — to see systems, patterns, and collective agreements objectively rather than emotionally. It governs individuation, innovation, rebellion against stagnation, and the awakening of future-oriented consciousness.

Souls with strong Aquarian emphasis often arrive feeling "different." The emotional body may feel atypical or detached. The mind moves quickly, abstractly, and non-linearly. There is often an early sense of not quite belonging — not because the soul is superior, but because it is **wired to operate outside the norm**. This difference is not accidental. It is the mechanism through which liberation becomes possible.

The paradox Aquarius must hold is this: true freedom often requires separation before it can serve connection. Detachment can awaken clarity, but isolation can harden into alienation. Aquarius evolves when it learns that liberation is not escape from humanity, but service to it — when authenticity becomes a gift offered back to the collective rather than a reason to stand apart. Aquarius fulfills its intention when the soul lives from truth rather than conditioning, and uses its difference not to reject the world, but to help it evolve.

AQUARIUS TWO FORCES

LIBERATION	EXILE
It is not rebellion for its own sake, and it is not emotional withdrawal. Liberation is coherence. It is the felt sense of being internally aligned with one's own frequency rather than contorted by collective expectation. In the body, liberation feels like space — emotional breathability, relaxed alertness, and a quiet clarity that does not require defense. The nervous system is regulated, not numb. The heart is open, but not entangled. In this state, Aquarius can love without losing itself. Thought is clear without becoming rigid. Perspective is wide without becoming detached from humanity. Choices are made from truth rather than approval, frequency rather than form, authenticity rather than tradition.	fear-based survival expression. Because Aquarian consciousness often develops ahead of its emotional environment, early expression frequently meets misunderstanding, rejection, or psychic overwhelm. The system adapts by pulling back. Detachment becomes protection. Distance becomes safety. The observing mind stays intact by disconnecting from the feeling body.

Every Aquarius placement must navigate a defining split: **Liberation versus Exile**. Both forces arise from the same core instinct — the need for energetic independence. Both can feel spacious, clear, and emotionally unburdened in the body. And because they feel similar somatically at first, they are often confused. Yet they lead to radically different outcomes for the soul.

Behaviorally, liberation shows up as principled action without dramatization, innovation without contempt for the past, and individuality that does not need to announce itself. The Aquarian individual participates in life while remaining internally sovereign. Difference becomes a contribution, not a shield.

Somatically, exile can feel deceptively similar to liberation at first. There is calm. There is quiet. There is distance from emotional turbulence. But underneath, there is contraction — a subtle withdrawal from intimacy, a numbing of sensation, a sense of being separate rather than spacious. Emotion is not absent; it is unprocessed. It lives beneath the surface, frozen in time.

Behaviorally, exile appears as emotional aloofness, intellectual superiority, avoidance of vulnerability, chronic observation without participation, or identifying as "different" in a way that hardens into isolation. Relationships may feel distant. Belonging feels impossible. The soul stands apart not from clarity, but from unresolved grief, fear, or overwhelm.

The evolutionary work of Aquarius is not to become more emotional. It is to **allow emotion to pass through the body without collapsing the observing field**. Objective awareness becomes liberating only when dissociation is no longer required. As trauma clears from the nervous system, Aquarius can remain present while holding vast awareness. True liberation does not come from leaving the body or humanity behind. It comes from inhabiting both fully — awake, sovereign, and connected. Consciousness is freed not by exile, but by embodiment.

Archetypal Patterns Aquarius

Wherever Aquarius appears, life repeatedly places the soul in situations that magnify the feeling of being different. Aquarius often finds itself on the outside of groups it technically belongs to — emotionally adjacent but not fully included, present but not mirrored. Friendships, families, schools, workplaces, even spiritual communities seem to reinforce the same experience: I don't quite fit here.

A defining Aquarian pattern is chronic otherness. Aquarius may feel like an observer rather than a participant, watching social dynamics from a slight distance. Conversations feel slightly off-frequency. Emotional exchanges feel either too dense or too scripted. Even when welcomed, Aquarius can sense an invisible gap — as if there's a pane of glass between its inner world and everyone else's.

Another recurring Aquarius situation is being placed into systems that feel outdated, illogical, or constricting. Rules feel arbitrary. Traditions feel hollow. Expectations feel misaligned with truth. Aquarius instinctively questions these structures, but often finds that doing so increases alienation. The response from the collective is subtle but consistent: Why can't you just be normal? Over time, Aquarius learns to withhold parts of itself — not to conform, but to survive.

Aquarius also repeatedly encounters emotional misunderstanding. Others may perceive Aquarius as cold, distant, or uninvested, when in reality Aquarius is overwhelmed by emotional saturation or operating at a different frequency. This misunderstanding reinforces detachment. The psyche concludes that closeness leads to misinterpretation, so distance feels safer.

Core Lessons Aquarius

Aquarius' core lesson begins when **difference stops being treated as a problem to solve**. The soul must recognize that what creates alienation is not an error in design — it is the source of its evolutionary function. The nervous system relaxes when Aquarius no longer forces resonance where none exists, no longer tries to contort itself into belonging, and no longer interprets nonconformity as failure.

What must be distinguished is **separation versus exile**. Separation is perceptual. It allows Aquarius to see systems, patterns, and futures clearly. Exile is emotional. It occurs when the body withdraws to avoid pain. Aquarius learns that distance does not require disconnection — and that clarity does not require numbness. What must be refined is Aquarius' relationship to embodiment. Observation alone is incomplete. Consciousness must be lived. The soul was never meant to remain outside of experience indefinitely. Aquarius begins to understand that it was not designed to fully blend into the present world — it is here to update it. Vision precedes integration.

What must be trusted is that authenticity is inherently connective when it is embodied. Aquarius does not serve the future by staying abstract or aloof. It serves it by becoming visible, warm, and human. This is where Leo becomes essential. Leo teaches Aquarius how to step out of observation and into expression — to let the heart participate, to allow difference to be lived rather than merely analyzed. As Aquarius integrates, connection returns — not through conformity, but through resonance. The individual no longer stands apart as an observer, nor dissolves into the collective. Aquarius becomes whole when difference is no longer defended or hidden, but expressed as a living contribution to the world.

Early Experience Aquarius

From early life, Aquarian souls often sense a quiet but persistent tension between who they are and what the environment expects them to be. There is an early awareness of difference — emotionally, intellectually, socially, or psychologically. Many Aquarians feel slightly out of sync with family systems or peers, as if they are tuned to a different frequency. This difference is rarely celebrated. More often, it is misunderstood.

As a result, an internal rebellion forms. Not always loud. Not always acted out. But deeply felt. A refusal to conform. A sense that blending in would require a kind of self-betrayal the psyche instinctively resists. Many Aquarians describe feeling like observers rather than full participants — present, perceptive, but never entirely included. This distance is not a flaw. It is adaptive. The soul disengages just enough to perceive itself without being overtaken by group conditioning.

For some, early life includes sudden disruptions: emotional instability, fractured family systems, unpredictable environments, or abrupt changes that break continuity. These experiences accelerate the Aquarian function. Attachment to old structures is interrupted early, forcing the psyche to adapt through objectivity, abstraction, and detachment. The nervous system learns: clarity requires distance.

Aquarius is ruled by Uranus — the archetype of lightning insight and quantum awareness. This creates a nervous system that processes reality in flashes rather than sequences. Information arrives as downloads, intuitive leaps, and pattern recognition others cannot follow. This psyche is not linear. It is electrical. When overstimulated, the Aquarian nervous system detaches — not from indifference, but from overload. Emotional fusion overwhelms perception. Distance restores clarity. This is not avoidance. It is regulation. Aquarius steps back not to disappear, but to come back online.
These early adaptations preserve authenticity. Later, the work becomes learning how to stay embodied and connected without losing that essential clarity.

The Polarity of Leo: Creative Selfhood
Where Aquarius awakens individuality through separation and perception, Leo teaches that uniqueness must be **lived**, not merely known. Insight without expression remains incomplete. Leo gives Aquarius the courage to be seen. It draws the Aquarian vision out of abstraction and into form. Ideas become actions. Values become choices. The future Aquarius perceives begins to take shape through embodied presence. Leo teaches Aquarius that leadership is not

domination or performance — it is visibility grounded in heart.

Through Leo, Aquarius learns how to let the heart participate. Emotional detachment softens into warmth. Objectivity becomes humanity. The Aquarian tendency to stand apart is tempered by Leo's willingness to stand *in*. Joy enters the equation, preventing rebellion from hardening into bitterness or superiority. Difference becomes creative rather than defensive.
Leo also teaches Aquarius that connection does not require conformity. Being seen does not mean being absorbed. Individuality does not disappear when it is expressed — it clarifies. When Aquarius integrates Leo, it no longer needs distance to preserve authenticity. Presence becomes safe. With Leo as medicine, the Aquarian mind joins the Aquarian heart. Vision gains vitality. Insight gains warmth. Innovation gains soul. Aquarius completes its evolutionary arc when it moves from observer to participant — when it allows its uniqueness to be expressed, embodied, and chosen again and again, not in opposition to the world, but in service to its becoming.

VIRGO
ARCHETYPAL INTENTION

The Soul Intention: To restore wholeness through compassion rather than self analysis. This archetype marks a critical turning point in evolution, where consciousness learns that clarity does not require criticism, and awareness does not need to become judgment. Virgo is not here to perfect life. It is here to *care for it*. At its deepest level, Virgo represents the soul's journey from self-correction to self-acceptance. Wherever Virgo appears in the chart, the soul is learning how to perceive reality accurately without using that perception to diminish itself or others. Virgo's sensitivity is extraordinary. It notices what is out of alignment, what is inefficient, what is wounded, what could function better. But this sensitivity is not meant to fix existence. It is meant to understand it with humility and care.

Virgo is necessary in the evolutionary cycle because awareness eventually turns inward. After the fire of selfhood and the air of vision, consciousness must learn how to live *inside* the human condition. Virgo teaches discernment in the realm of daily life, embodiment, health, service, and integration. It grounds awareness into the practical realities of being human without losing reverence for the whole.

The paradox Virgo must hold is subtle and demanding: the same perception that allows healing can also create harm. When fear is present, Virgo's discernment hardens into self-criticism, control, and chronic dissatisfaction. The soul becomes trapped in an endless loop of improvement, mistaking worthiness for flawlessness. When trust is present, that same perception becomes compassion. Attention becomes care. Discernment becomes devotion. Virgo's evolution is not about becoming better. It is about becoming kinder — especially toward the self. When Virgo awakens, analysis softens into empathy, service becomes sacred rather than self-erasing, and healing replaces fixing. Virgo fulfills its intention when it learns that wholeness is not achieved by eliminating imperfection, but by **meeting imperfection with understanding**.

Every Virgo placement must navigate a subtle but decisive split: **Perfectionism versus Discernment**. Both forces arise from the same source — heightened sensitivity and awareness. Both notice what is out of alignment. Both seek order, clarity, and improvement. The difference is not moral. It is somatic. One contracts the body into vigilance. The other relaxes the body into presence.

VIRGO TWO FORCES

DISCERNMENT	PERFECTIONISM
is Virgo's soul-aligned expression. It emerges when the nervous system learns that sensitivity does not require self-attack. Discernment is the capacity to perceive clearly without collapsing into judgment. The body feels grounded and steady. Attention rests rather than scans. There is space between noticing and reacting.	is Virgo's fear-based survival strategy. It develops when early environments — quietly or explicitly — communicated that love, safety, or belonging depended on being correct, helpful, calm, competent, or good. The nervous system learned that mistakes were dangerous, that disorder led to punishment or abandonment, and that vigilance was required to prevent harm

Somatically, discernment feels calm and receptive. The body trusts its ability to meet reality without immediately correcting it. Awareness is precise, but not sharp. There is softness around perception. Truth is named without urgency. Discernment listens before it intervenes. Behaviorally, discernment shows up as accurate perception paired with compassion, service that flows from presence rather than obligation, skill without self-erasure, humility without shame, and the ability to refine reality gently over time. Virgo still improves systems, supports healing, and offers service — but not at the expense of its own humanity. Effort becomes devotion rather than self-sacrifice.

Somatically, perfectionism feels tight and alert. The body is always slightly braced. Attention scans for error before it happens. There is pressure in the chest, jaw, or gut — a sense of needing to stay ahead of life. Thought loops focus on what could go wrong, what should be improved, what must be fixed now. This creates chronic self-monitoring. Behaviorally, perfectionism expresses as harsh inner critique, compulsive fixing of self or others, people-pleasing disguised as service, over-preparation, fear of exposure, and equating worth with usefulness. Help is offered not from overflow, but from anxiety. Care becomes control. Perfectionism does regulate the nervous system — but only temporarily. The cost is intimacy with the self. Awareness turns inward as punishment rather than understanding, slowly fracturing the soul.

Both forces involve care. Both involve attention. The difference lies in **what attention is used for**. Perfectionism uses awareness to regulate fear. Discernment uses awareness to support life. Virgo evolves when it learns this reminder in the body: *I can see clearly without hurting myself.* When attention becomes an act of love rather than control, Virgo's greatest gift emerges — not perfection, but healing.

Archetypal Patterns Virgo

One of the most misunderstood dynamics of Virgo and the Sixth House is the presence of an **invisible, pre-rational guilt** as Jeffrey Wolf Green teaches. This guilt cannot be traced to a single mistake, moral failure, or traumatic event. It does not respond to reassurance or logic. It simply exists as a background frequency in the nervous system. A quiet sense that something is off. Unfinished. Slightly wrong.

Because the Sixth House carries the archetype of purification, this unnamed guilt automatically implies its shadow: impurity. The psyche subtly assumes that something within the self is contaminated or unworthy of ease. Once this assumption takes root, a quiet compulsion toward atonement emerges. Life becomes something that must be corrected before it can be enjoyed.

This is where the Virgo pattern becomes self-reinforcing. Virgo unconsciously withholds care from itself — not because it does not know what would help, but because support feels undeserved. Rest is delayed. Pleasure is postponed. Nourishment is earned rather than allowed. There is an inner logic that says: *Once I fix this... once I'm better... once I'm more prepared... then I can relax.* Discomfort becomes familiar. Strain feels necessary. Ease feels suspicious.

As a result, Virgo repeatedly finds itself in states of mild-to-moderate dysfunction. Life is rarely in full collapse, but it is rarely settled either. There is always something to optimize, something to correct, something slightly out of place. Feeling behind. Overwhelmed. Not ready yet. These states are not accidental. They activate Virgo's core function: analysis.

And analysis provides relief. When life feels off, Virgo knows what to do — examine, refine, improve. Awareness increases. Insight sharpens. Patterns are identified. For a moment, the nervous system settles because attention has found a task. But the improvement attempt often reinforces the original belief: *something is wrong with me.* Guilt returns. The cycle restarts.

This creates a hidden loop:

guilt → self-denial → crisis → analysis → awareness → attempted self-improvement → guilt

Another Virgo pattern is chronic self-interruption. Even when life begins to stabilize, Virgo may unconsciously introduce friction — taking on too much, neglecting basic needs, over-committing, or tightening standards — to recreate the familiar tension that justifies vigilance. Calm feels unearned. Functioning well feels temporary. The nervous system remains oriented toward fixing rather than inhabiting.

Over time, this pattern can lead to burnout, health issues, anxiety, or a sense of being perpetually "in process." Virgo may be admired for competence and reliability while privately feeling like a project that is never finished.

These patterns are not flaws. They are adaptations. The soul learned that attention keeps things from falling apart. The tragedy is not that Virgo notices too much — it is that it learned to turn that noticing against itself.

Virgo begins to heal when care is no longer used as currency for worthiness. When nourishment is given without prerequisites. When attention becomes an act of kindness rather than correction. The archetype evolves when the nervous system learns a new truth: **nothing needs to be purified before it can be loved**

The Early Experience Virgo

When Virgo is wounded or unbalanced, one formative experience shapes the psyche early: its natural capacity to perceive, discern, and notice subtle truth was **disregarded, dismissed, or misunderstood**. The child sensed what was off long before anyone else did — emotional incongruence, unspoken tension, inefficiency, misalignment — but lacked the authority, language, or permission to trust that perception. What the body knew could not be named or validated.

This creates a crucial internal pivot. If the environment does not acknowledge what the child perceives, the psyche draws a painful conclusion: *If something feels wrong, it must be me.* Rather than trusting perception, Virgo internalizes it. Awareness turns inward. Discernment becomes self-monitoring. Sensitivity becomes self-correction.

From the nervous system's perspective, this was adaptive. Hyper-attunement kept chaos manageable. Becoming useful reduced friction. Being prepared prevented reprimand or rejection. Over time, the body learned that safety depended on being good, helpful, quiet, competent, and correct. Love became conditional on usefulness. Belonging became something to earn rather than something given.

This early adaptation explains why Virgo so often confuses care with criticism. The child was not taught how to rest inside awareness — only how to apply it. There was no space to simply be. Only room to improve.

As an adult, this shows up as chronic self-surveillance, difficulty receiving care without guilt, and an inner voice that withholds approval until some invisible standard is met. The body remains alert, scanning for what might be wrong next.

This is not a flaw of character. It is the residue of unmirrored sensitivity. Virgo did not become critical because it is harsh. It became critical because its perception needed a place to land — and it landed on itself.

Healing begins when Virgo learns that perception does not require punishment. Awareness does not need to hurt. The very sensitivity that once became self-attack is the same sensitivity that, when met with compassion, becomes medicine.

Core Lessons Virgo

Virgo's pattern begins to shift the moment **crisis is no longer treated as evidence of failure**, but as information. A signal. A diagnostic tool that reveals unconscious dynamics rather than a sentence to be endured. When Virgo stops asking, *What did I do wrong?* and begins asking, *What is being shown?*, the nervous system softens. Attention becomes curious instead of corrective. The key lesson is **rhythm**. Virgo does not heal by constant analysis, nor by relentless action. Too much reflection collapses vitality into rumination. Too much action without reflection recreates the same distortions in new form. Healing occurs when Virgo learns to alternate consciously between observation and engagement — to let insight inform movement, and movement refine insight. Balance restores trust in the self.

What must be distinguished is **discernment versus self-judgment**. Discernment clarifies reality. Self-judgment contracts it. Virgo learns that seeing clearly does not require punishment. Awareness does not need to hurt in order to be effective. What must be refined is Virgo's relationship to the body. The body is not a problem to manage or a system to correct — it is the **instrument of consciousness**. Sensation carries truth before thought does. Fatigue, tension, and illness are not moral failures; they are messages asking for recalibration.

What must be trusted is that wholeness does not require perfection. Virgo is here to integrate what is real, release what is distorted, refine without rejecting, and serve without disappearing. When Virgo stops using improvement as a way to earn worth, its true gift emerges.
Virgo is not here to control the world. It is here to clarify it — through discernment, humility, presence, skill, and devotion to what actually matters.

The Pisces Polarity:
Virgo completes its evolutionary arc through its polarity: **Pisces**. Where Virgo refines, Pisces dissolves. Where Virgo analyzes, Pisces trusts. This is not a contradiction — it is a correction of imbalance. Pisces does not negate Virgo's precision; it **elevates it**. Pisces teaches Virgo to see the forest for the trees. It restores a sense of meaning when attention becomes trapped in minutiae. Through Pisces, Virgo learns that not everything that is felt must be fixed, and not everything that is imperfect is broken. Compassion enters where correction once ruled. Mercy softens precision. Trust replaces vigilance.

Without Pisces, Virgo risks becoming a workhorse — endlessly improving systems, tending wounds, managing details, yet losing touch with why any of it matters. Service becomes obligation. Refinement becomes self-punishment. Pisces reintroduces the sacred. It reminds Virgo that every practical act is also a spiritual one when performed with presence and love. Cleaning becomes care. Service becomes devotion. Skill becomes prayer.

Pisces also teaches Virgo surrender. Not collapse, not passivity — but release. Release of the belief that awareness must carry responsibility for everything it sees. Release of the need to justify rest. Release of guilt as a motivator. When Pisces is integrated, Virgo learns to rest in uncertainty without anxiety, to allow life to unfold without constant management. Most importantly, Pisces gives Virgo the capacity to **trust** — trust the body, trust timing, trust that healing does not always require effort. With this trust, refinement no longer becomes punishment. Discernment no longer wounds. Service no longer erases the self.

Virgo becomes whole when precision is guided by compassion, when effort is infused with faith, and when care is offered not as atonement, but as love.

ARCHETYPAL INTENTION

The Soul Intention: To reconnect consciousness with a reality that does not depend on form, identity, role, structure, or time. This archetype is the closing movement of the zodiacal cycle, where the soul remembers that it is not the body, not the personality, and not the story it has lived — but the awareness that existed before all of it. Pisces is necessary in the evolutionary cycle because, without it, consciousness would remain trapped in form. The ego would believe it is the source. The soul would forget its origin. Pisces reopens the the innate awareness that there is something beyond the ego, beyond even the soul's individual storyline. This impulse is what allows human consciousness to perceive the presence of a greater intelligence moving through life itself. It is how the soul remembers the God/dess not as an idea, but as a living current within.

A Pisces-structured nervous system is porous by design. It does not read the environment — it absorbs it. Emotions, atmospheres, unspoken wounds, ancestral residue, and subtle realms move through the body before language ever forms. This sensitivity is not pathology. It is access. But without grounding and discernment, it creates confusion: *Where do I end and others begin? Is this intuition or trauma? Is this truth or fantasy?*

Here lies Pisces' central paradox: the same permeability that grants access to the divine can also dissolve the self. The same sensitivity that opens timeless awareness can erase boundaries needed for incarnation. Pisces must learn to surrender illusion without surrendering embodiment. To dissolve what is false without disappearing entirely. At its highest expression, Pisces allows consciousness to perceive simultaneously: ego, soul, and the greater field of being — not as concepts, but as lived reality. Pisces completes the evolutionary arc by teaching that form is temporary, essence is eternal, and love is the thread that connects all states of existence.

Every Pisces placement must navigate a subtle but profound split: **Union versus Fantasy**. Both forces arise from the same source — the transcendental impulse. Both involve sensitivity, permeability, and contact with realities beyond ordinary perception. And because they feel similar in the body at first, they are often confused. Yet they lead the soul in opposite directions.

PISCES TWO FORCES

UNION	FANTASY
Pisces in its soul-aligned expression. It is transcendence with embodiment. In this state, consciousness expands without abandoning form. The world is not rejected or escaped — it is included within a larger field of awareness. The nervous system is open, but regulated. Permeable, but coherent.	fear-based survival expression. It occurs when the desire to unite with its source is activated without grounding, containment, or nervous system regulation. Consciousness expands faster than the body can hold. Boundaries blur before coherence is established.

Somatically, union feels soft and grounded at the same time. There is a sense of being held by something vast without losing orientation in the body. Breath deepens. Time slows. Intuition arrives quietly, without urgency or distortion. There is no need to convince, escape, or prove. Knowing is immediate and intimate. Behaviorally, union expresses as compassion that arises naturally rather than morally, faith that is lived rather than believed, surrender without passivity, and intuition that guides action instead of replacing it. Pisces becomes a bridge between worlds — able to translate timeless truth into human meaning. Personal will aligns with Higher Will, not through obedience, but through resonance. Life becomes co-creative rather than chaotic.

Somatically, fantasy feels like flooding or fading. The body becomes vague, unanchored, or overwhelmed. Emotions arrive without edges. Sensations lack orientation. There may be fatigue, dissociation, or a drifting sense of unreality. Instead of being held by something greater, the self feels like it is disappearing into it. Behaviorally, fantasy shows up as confusion between inner perception and external reality, idealization followed by disillusionment, spiritual bypassing, projection, escapism, withdrawal, or emotional enmeshment. Meaning dissolves without replacement. The soul touches something vast but cannot integrate it, leading to collapse rather than revelation.

This is not weakness. It is a timing issue. Pisces does not fail here — it opens too quickly. Without Virgo's discernment and Saturnian containment, transcendence becomes disorientation rather than liberation.

The evolutionary task of Pisces is not to retreat from the infinite, but to **stay present while touching it**. Union requires structure. Grounding. Rhythm. Embodiment. When the nervous system can hold expanded awareness, Pisces fulfills its role: reminding consciousness of what is eternal while still inhabiting the human experience. True transcendence does not dissolve the self into nothingness. It dissolves illusion — while allowing life, love, and form to continue, illuminated from within.

Archetypal Patterns Pisces

Wherever Pisces appears, life repeatedly places the soul inside experiences where reality feels thinner than it looks. Pisces perceives possibilities, emotional truths, timelines, and relational potentials that exist beyond the immediate moment. These are not fantasies. They are genuine perceptions of what *could* exist. The difficulty is that Pisces initially assumes what is perceived can be entered directly — without time, structure, or embodiment.

A defining Piscean pattern is living in contact with **what is possible** rather than what is presently lived. Pisces often carries the sense that there are other worlds, other versions of love, other ways of being that feel more real than this one. Relationships may feel timeless or karmic. Callings may feel divinely ordained. Encounters arrive with the sensation of recognition — *I know you from somewhere beyond this life*. The soul is touching something eternal, but the human life has not yet built the container to hold it. This creates a recurring pattern of disillusionment.

Pisces sees the **highest expression** in people — their essence rather than their current capacity. It loves the soul, not the personality. And so it assumes that what is true in essence must be available now. Reality eventually contradicts the vision. Human fear, limitation, immaturity, or circumstance intervenes. Heartbreak follows — not because love was false, but because it could not yet exist in form. This is one of Pisces' most painful lessons: knowing what is real in essence, but being unable to live it in time.

Another recurring Piscean pattern is the sense that one could simply "go" somewhere else — another place, another frequency, another life where safety, belonging, or meaning already exist. This is not shallow escapism. It is the soul remembering that reality is not confined to this plane. But without grounding, this remembrance becomes dissatisfaction with incarnation itself. The body feels heavy. Time feels cruel. Limits feel like betrayal.

Pisces may repeatedly build inner worlds, spiritual ideals, or relational fantasies that feel truer than lived experience. These worlds sustain the soul — until they collapse. When they do, Pisces feels emptied and unanchored. The grief is existential. It is not just the loss of something loved. It is the loss of the place where meaning lived.

This creates a familiar cycle:
vision → idealization → attempted merging → disillusionment → withdrawal → longing → renewed seeking

Over time, this pattern can lead to exhaustion, spiritual despair, or a sense of being perpetually homeless in reality. Pisces is not confused because it sees too little. It suffers because it sees too much, too soon. The evolutionary invitation of Pisces is not to abandon vision, but to **learn timing**. To stay present while truth unfolds slowly. To allow what is eternal to enter form through patience, boundaries, and embodiment. When Pisces learns to remain here while sensing beyond, it becomes what it was always meant to be: a bridge between worlds, rather than a soul lost between them.

Early Life Experiences Pisces
When Pisces is wounded or unintegrated, early life is often shaped by **emotional incoherence**. One or both caregivers may be physically present but psychically absent — emotionally unavailable, overwhelmed, addicted, depressed, or living inside their own form of escape. For the Pisces child, this creates a world where safety is inconsistent and meaning feels unstable. Nothing is solid enough to rest in. The Pisces nervous system responds exactly as it is designed to. It absorbs everything. Emotion, atmosphere, unspoken pain, confusion, longing — none of it is filtered. There are no boundaries yet. The child does not distinguish between what belongs to them and what belongs to others. Survival depends on attunement, not protection. Hyper-sensitivity becomes the only way to stay oriented.

Because Pisces is born with an innate orientation toward unity and goodness, it often begins life believing that people are fundamentally loving and well-intentioned. This is not naïveté. It is innocence. The soul recognizes essence before it understands limitation. When reality contradicts this — through neglect, addiction, betrayal, volatility, or inconsistency — the shock is profound. This disillusionment is not incidental. It is initiatory. The soul learns early that external reality cannot reliably provide safety, coherence, or meaning. When caregivers escape their own inner emptiness through substances, fantasy, avoidance, or distraction, the Pisces child is left inside an emotional void it cannot name. Meaning evaporates before it has fully formed. Fantasy, imagination, spiritual longing, and inner worlds become refuge. The child learns how to leave without leaving. Consciousness drifts. Identity becomes porous. The self feels fluid rather than anchored.

Pisces becomes vulnerable to deception — not from lack of intelligence, but from leading with empathy. It sees who others *could* be and assumes essence will manifest. When it doesn't, the heartbreak is devastating. Forgiveness comes easily. Discernment comes later. This early adaptation preserves the soul's openness. The work of adulthood is learning how to stay — without losing the doorway to the infinite.

The Polarity Path: Virgo
Pisces completes its evolutionary arc through its polarity: **Virgo**. Virgo is not here to correct Pisces or pull it out of mystery. Virgo is here to *anchor* it. Where Pisces dissolves, Virgo contains. Where Pisces

senses, Virgo discerns. Together, they allow transcendence to become livable. Virgo teaches Pisces a crucial truth: not everything you sense is meant to be merged with. Not every vision is meant to be lived. Not every feeling is truth. This is not a dismissal of intuition — it is its refinement. Discernment does not negate perception; it stabilizes it. Without discernment, intuition overwhelms the nervous system. With it, intuition becomes guidance.

Virgo also teaches Pisces that structure does not limit the infinite — it gives it a place to land. Ritual, rhythm, boundaries, and practical care are not betrayals of spirituality. They are how spirit enters form. Virgo grounds Pisces' dreams so they can exist in reality rather than dissolve into fantasy or longing. As Virgo integrates, Pisces learns to stay present in the body while remaining open to the unseen. Emotional boundaries become possible without hardening. Compassion becomes practical instead of sacrificial. Service becomes embodied rather than self-erasing. Vision slows enough to be integrated.

This polarity completes a profound realization: **the body is not a prison — it is the vessel for consciousness**. Pisces does not lose access to the divine by becoming grounded. It gains the capacity to live it. Pisces' evolutionary journey in every lifetime is this: dissolve what is false, embody what is real, merge with the divine without disappearing. Pisces is not here to escape the world. It is here to spiritualize it — through presence, intuition, compassion, service, and a willingness to remain incarnate while touching the eternal.

6 THE PLANETS

The foundation of this book is that your life runs on unconscious patterns, and this chapter is where you begin to name them. You're not here to memorize archetypes or decode symbols — you're here to meet yourself. Your chart is not a personality profile. It's a dynamic pattern map. The planets, signs, and houses don't just describe *who you are* — they reveal *how your soul has learned to survive*, where it repeats, and how it's trying to evolve.

The Most Important Principle in This Book
Your entire blueprint is organized around Pluto. Pluto is not "one planet among many." It is the root system. It represents the original soul intent, the core survival intelligence, and the karmic material your consciousness is here to metabolize. Every other planet functions as an expression, adaptation, or branch of that initial soul intent. Think of Pluto as the underground current. The rest of the chart grows out of it. This is why you do not read planets in isolation in this work. You read them as pattern functions serving a deeper evolutionary drive.

Start by pulling up your **natal chart**. You'll need your exact birth time, date, and location. If you don't already have your chart, you can generate one for free using tools like Astro.com, AstroSeek, or any reputable astrology app. Make sure you're looking at a whole chart wheel — not just a list of signs or traits. You'll need to see planetary placements, houses, and aspects.

The Planetary Functions at a Glance
Use this framework as an orientation, not a checklist.
Pluto — Core Soul Intent & Survival Intelligence Function: What the soul is here to confront, transform, and reclaim. Pluto holds the

deepest unconscious material. It shows where power, fear, control, and survival patterns live. Everything else in the chart organizes itself around this axis. Pluto is not about choice. It is about inevitability and evolution.

PLANETARY CONSCIOUSNESS & SOUL INTENT
Why No Planet Lives in Only One Pattern

At this stage, it's important to release the idea that planets belong neatly inside categories. While certain planets are more closely associated with belief, somatic memory, or evolutionary timing, no planet operates in isolation. The psyche is not modular. It is relational.

Planets are not traits or symbols. They are living fields of psychic and spiritual energy — instruments through which consciousness experiences itself in form. If the sign is the *nature of the dynamic* and the house is the *stage* then the planet is the vehicle driving the interaction. Planets act. They initiate. They respond. They evolve. Below is a highly generalized expression of each of the planets function, and how they become players in your evolutionary design. A planet is not what you *are*. It is how energy *moves through you*.

A single planetary activation can: trigger a belief pattern, activate a somatic response, coincide with a timing initiation. Depending on how it interacts with the rest of the chart and the current phase of life. So instead of placing planets into fixed boxes, we will approach them as forms of consciousness — each one contributing a specific function to the soul's evolutionary intent. Pluto remains the root. But every planet is a branch — expressing, adapting, and responding to that deeper current. We extensively cover the moon in its own chapter, as well as

LIFE FORCE, HOW YOU GIVE LIFE PURPOSE, EXPRESSION

How the Sun Gives Purpose to Experience. The Sun's sign, house, and aspects describe how you integrate experience into identity. Not what happens to you — but how you *make something of it*. The Sun organizes experience into meaning and direction. It is the part of consciousness that asks: "What is this shaping me into?" This is why the Sun is so closely tied to purpose. Purpose is not something you choose abstractly. It emerges from how you metabolize what life brings you.

Most people do not evolve through comfort. They evolve through friction, disruption, and challenge. The Sun shows *how* you learn from these moments and how you weave them into your nature rather than being defined or broken by them. In this way, the Sun does not prevent crisis. It gives crisis direction.

Sign	**How You Integrate Experience Into Identity and Purpose** The Sun's sign reveals **how your consciousness organizes lived experience into identity** — and why your soul chose that particular style of becoming. The Sun's sign shows the instinctual way you *make sense of who you are* through what happens to you. It describes how you integrate challenge, crisis, achievement, and failure into a coherent sense of purpose — often before awareness enters the body. This is not about personality traits. It is about **identity reflex**.
House	**Where You Integrate Experience Into Identity and Purpose** The Sun's house shows the area of life where you are forged through experience. This is where life repeatedly applies pressure so that identity can form, refine, and mature. It is not where things are easiest — it is where you are asked to *become someone* through what you live. This is where your soul learns: who you are through challenge, how to integrate crisis into character, how to give purpose to what happens to you. The Sun does not describe events. It describes how you metabolize them into selfhood.
Aspects	***What Shapes the Process*** The **aspects** to the Sun show *how smooth or confrontational* that process feels. Supportive aspects build confidence and continuity. Challenging aspects create crisis that forces growth. Either way, the Sun becomes strong not by avoiding difficulty, but by **making meaning out of it**.

♂ MARS ♂

DESIRE, ACTION, AND THE CONSEQUENCES OF MISALIGNMENT

Desire, Action, and the Consequences of Misalignment. Mars represents the soul's desire function — the force that moves energy into action. It is the point where wanting becomes doing, where instinct turns into movement, and where inner truth demands expression in the external world. Mars is the lower octave of Pluto. Pluto holds the soul's deep evolutionary intent. Mars is how that intent attempts to *act itself out* in daily life. Because of this, Mars is never neutral. Every action you take is either: aligned with the soul's evolution or defending an outdated survival identity. There is no middle ground.

Mars determines whether you recreate the past or move beyond it.

Sign	How Action Instinctively Expresses
	Mars' sign reveals how action moves through you before awareness intervenes. It describes the instinctual style your life force uses to assert, defend, pursue, or withdraw when desire is activated. This is not about temperament or motivation. It is about reflexive movement. When Mars is unconscious, its sign runs automatically. Action happens faster than thought. The body mobilizes before the mind can evaluate whether the movement is aligned or reactive. This is why Mars is so closely tied to consequence.
House	Where Action Is Repeatedly Tested
	Mars' house shows where your actions are repeatedly challenged, corrected, and refined over time. This is the area of life where you are forced to learn *how* to act — not once, but again and again. This is not where you act perfectly. It is where action has consequences. The Mars house reveals where desire meets resistance, where assertion creates feedback, and where impulsive or misaligned action eventually produces crisis until awareness is brought in.
Aspects	How Action Is Conditioned, Distorted, or Refined
	Mars' aspects show what interferes with, intensifies, redirects, or matures your capacity to act. They describe how the desire function has been shaped by experience — and why action may feel conflicted, delayed, explosive, or unusually consequential. Aspects do not describe *how much* Mars you have. They describe what Mars has to contend

	with. This is where action becomes complicated.

When Mars is aligned with the soul, action leads forward — even when it's uncomfortable. When Mars is misaligned, action becomes reactive, compulsive, and crisis-generating. Mars does not cause events. It takes action. When Mars is driven by fear, it acts in service of survival rather than truth. The ego uses Mars to protect identity, avoid loss, or maintain control — even when that identity is no longer aligned with the soul. Life begins to feel dramatic not because fate is cruel, but because Mars is recreating unresolved Plutonic material. This is when people experience: repeated crises, volatile relationships, sudden losses, external confrontations that mirror internal conflict.

♀ VENUS ♀
FEELING FUNCTION INNER VALUE →
RELATIONAL MIRROR → ATTRACTION OUTCOME

as a Three-Layered Consciousness

Venus is the function through which we **feel**. Not emotion. Feeling. Venus governs the immediate, pre-verbal registration that occurs the moment we encounter anything: a person, a tone of voice, a room, an idea, a memory, a possibility. Before the mind interprets, before the emotional body reacts, Venus registers. It answers quietly and instantly: this is pleasant, this is unsafe, this draws me in, this repels me, this resonates, this does not. This first, subtle response belongs to Venus. Emotions come later. Emotions are layered, complex reactions that arise after feeling has already occurred. They involve memory, attachment, fear, hope, and narrative. Venus is faster than emotion. Quieter. More immediate. It does not explain itself. It simply registers value.

This is why Venus is so often misunderstood. People think Venus is about romance or desire, but those are secondary expressions. At its core, Venus is the sensory and energetic interface between consciousness and experience. It is the inner sensor that tracks safety, beauty, attraction, resonance, harmony, and worth.

As the lower octave of Neptune, Venus is where the soul's longing for union first becomes perceptible in the body. Neptune seeks total dissolution into the divine. Venus seeks connection in form. Neptune longs for transcendence. Venus asks, *does this feel right to move toward?* Venus is how the infinite begins to choose.

Venus does not operate through a single sign. Venus is a relational consciousness that unfolds through three distinct layers:
1. **The Inner Value System** (the Venus root)
2. **The Relational Expression** (how you meet the other)
3. **The Attraction Outcome** (what you magnetize when integrated)

Venus as Inner Consciousness: Taurus
In its inner expression, Taurus, Venus governs the relationship you have with yourself. This is not self-love as an idea. It is self-relation as sensation. Venus in Taurus describes: what you notice in yourself, what you criticize or reject, what you soften toward, what you allow pleasure to reach, what you deny yourself access to. This is where value is embodied or withheld. Taurus Venus reveals how safe it feels to inhabit your own body, to enjoy simplicity, to stay present without reaching outward for validation. When Venus in Taurus is unconscious, value must be reinforced through attachment, comfort, or possession. When conscious, value is intrinsic and felt somatically. This inner Venus is the foundation. Nothing external can stabilize what is not first sensed internally.

When Venus is unconscious, these layers fragment. When Venus matures, they align. To understand Venus correctly, you must read it across its polarity and its evolutionary axis, not as a trait.

Venus as Relational Consciousness: Libra
In its outer expression, Libra, Venus governs how we meet the other. Here, Venus describes: who you magnetize, how you bond, what you tolerate, how you give and receive affection, how harmony is maintained or avoided, what you unconsciously invite into relationship. Libra Venus does not simply show preference. It reveals **mirroring**. The relational field becomes a reflection of the inner Venus state. How you treat yourself is echoed back through the people you attract, the dynamics you enter, and the behaviors you excuse. Venus does not attract what you want. It attracts what matches your internal valuation. This is why relationship patterns repeat until Venus consciousness shifts. The outer field cannot

change until the inner sensor recalibrates.

Sign	**How Value and Attraction Operate Automatically** Venus by sign describes how you instinctively register value and attraction before awareness enters the body. This is not about taste, romance, or preference. It is about what feels worthy, safe, or desirable automatically without thinking, without choosing, without justification. Venus' sign answers the quiet, pre-verbal question: Does this feel like something I can move toward? You feel this before you know why. This is why attraction patterns often repeat even when the mind wants something different. Venus is operating below cognition. It is responding from an internal value imprint formed early and reinforced over time. When Venus is unconscious, its sign runs automatically and attracts mirrors of that value system. When Venus becomes conscious, the same sign becomes a tool rather than a reflex.
House	**Where Value, Worth, and Tolerance Are Tested** Venus' house shows where value becomes lived experience. This is the area of life where worth is reinforced, negotiated, compromised, or reclaimed through real interaction with the world. This is not where things are easiest. It is where your sense of value is activated.
Aspects	**Pluto** → feeling function until attraction becomes compulsive, exposing where sensing value and resonance is fused with survival, control, or fear of loss. **Saturn** → Saturn restricts Venus' capacity to feel pleasure or connection until value can be embodied without dependency, obligation, or self-denial. **Mars** → Mars charges Venus' feeling responses with urgency, causing attraction or aversion to arise reactively rather than from settled, embodied resonance. **Moon** → The Moon entangles Venus' felt responses with emotional memory, causing present attraction to be colored by past attachment and safety patterns. **Mercury** → Mercury overlays Venus' sensing function with interpretation, often replacing direct feeling with narrative, comparison, or mental justification. **Jupiter** → Jupiter expands Venus' field of attraction, magnifying desire, expectation, and idealization beyond what the body can realistically embody. **Neptune** → Neptune dissolves Venus' discernment, blurring feeling with fantasy so attraction is experienced as longing, projection, or imagined union rather than embodied resonance. **Uranus** → Uranus destabilizes Venus' feeling patterns, interrupting habitual attraction so value can be re-sensed outside conditioning

	and repetition.

☿ MERCURY ☿

COMMUNICATION, THINKING, LEARNING, LOGIC

How You Process and Structure Reality

Sign	How You Intellectually Organize Experience Mercury's sign reveals how your mind creates order out of reality — and why your soul chose that style of perception. It's about how your consciousness processes, names, and structures the world, and what evolutionary purpose that serves. Each Mercury sign reflects a distinct cognitive orientation — a way of linking thought to thought, forming language, and constructing your personal logic system. But beneath that mental style is an archetypal intent: a soul-level reason for seeing and speaking the way you do. Ask: "What is the soul trying to remember, restore, or relearn through the way it thinks and speaks?"
House	Where You Seek Intellectual Clarity The house Mercury occupies reveals where in life you try to make sense of things. This is where your mind is most active, curious, and in need of organization. If Mercury is in the 7th house, you seek clarity through dialogue. In the 12th, through solitude and metaphysics. In the 10th, through public systems and career mastery. This is the arena where your belief patterns are built through logic and deduction, based on direct experience.
Aspects	What Shapes Your Perception Mercury aspects show the core influences — both internal and external — that condition how you process reality. Do you struggle to trust your mind (Mercury-Saturn)? Do you bypass rationality (Mercury-Neptune)? These aspects point to karmic contracts around communication, learning, and cognition. They reveal the kinds of people, systems, or psychological defenses that shape your thinking — and the distortions you must unravel to reclaim your own voice.

JUPITER ♃ ♃

HOW YOU DERIVE MEANING AND CONSTRUCT BELIEF

Sign	How You Intuit the Larger Truth: reflects the way your soul seeks meaning, faith, and philosophical orientation. This is the intuitive, inductive mind — not the mind that names, but the one that knows. Jupiter in Sagittarius expands through freedom and cosmic laws. In Scorpio, through emotional truth and depth. In Capricorn, through structure, discipline, and earned wisdom. This is how your consciousness grasps what it all means, even when there's no evidence — the framework of faith that shapes your worldview.
House	Where You Construct and Test Your Beliefs: the area of life where you're meant to pursue wisdom and experience. This is where you explore, question, grow — where beliefs are tested and reshaped. If Jupiter is in the 9th, this might be literal study. In the 4th, it's meaning through family history. In the 6th, through service and refinement. Jupiter seeks the whole picture. This is where your soul is asking: What's the higher meaning of this?
Aspects	What Shapes Your Concept of Truth Jupiter aspects reveal the energies that influence how you form beliefs. If you have Jupiter square the Moon, emotional security may distort belief. With Neptune, belief may substitute for clarity. These aspects show where belief becomes inflated, bypassed, dogmatic, or disillusioned — and where your soul is being asked to evolve from projection to truth.

UNIVERSAL *timing*

The planets that are typically expressing through the evolutionary cycle of your soul are going to be referenced below. However these planets are still actively functioning and participating with the interplay between the planets.

♇ PLUTO ♇

THE SOUL, SEPERATING DESIRES, EVOLUTION

A Note on Evolutionary Astrology Sources
Jeffrey Wolf Green's work on Pluto and the Soul is foundational to the field of Evolutionary Astrology. His teachings — along with Deva Green's expansions on them — explore Pluto in far greater technical, philosophical, and karmic depth than this book intends to cover. Their work is referenced in the back of this text for readers who want a complete understanding of the evolutionary paradigm. What you will find here is not a replication of their material, but my lived experience of Pluto's function — how it has revealed itself through crisis, compulsion, trauma repetition, and ultimate transformation. My interpretation comes from embodiment, not doctrine. It is observational, experiential, and rooted in the terrain of the unconscious patterns I have personally had to confront.

With that in mind, here is the simplified method I offer to help you identify your Pluto pattern: It is a planet you feel — in the places where life forces you to change. It is the undercurrent of your entire incarnation, the gravitational pull behind your desires, your fears, your compulsions, and every cycle of destruction and rebirth you will experience. Pluto symbolizes the part of your soul that remembers what your conscious mind cannot. It holds: the original contract you came in with, what remains unfinished from previous lifetimes, the emotional terrain you must walk before reclaiming your power, the patterns you repeat because your body still confuses them with survival.

Pluto exposes what has been buried, denied, or survived rather than integrated. It reveals darkness not to shame it, but to purify it. Pluto will not allow consciousness to evolve while emotional truth is avoided. This is why Pluto feels obsessive, intense, or annihilating. It is dismantling false identity so something truer can emerge. Pluto shows why you keep doing what you do — even when you know better, even when it hurts, even when you try to stop. To locate your personal soul blueprint:

| **Sign** | The Nature of Your Core Soul Pattern Pluto's sign describes |

	the type of emotional, psychological, and evolutionary pattern your soul compulsively repeats. This is not surface-level personality. This is the ancestral, karmic, deep-rooted instinct you reenact until you become conscious of it.
House	Where Your Soul Is Trying to Evolve Pluto's house shows the arena of life where evolution is non-negotiable. This is where crisis forces you inward. Where compulsion becomes transformation. Where you lose power until you learn how to hold it correctly.
Aspects	Who Activates Your Deepest Transformations Pluto aspects reveal the people, transits, relationships, and internal conflicts that trigger your core evolutionary work. These aspects don't create the wound — they expose it.

♄ SATURN ♄

THE STRUCTURAL NATURE OF THE SOUL'S CONSCIOUSNESS

Saturn shapes the structure of your consciousness in each lifetime — the framework through which every other archetype will express itself. Saturn determines the limit of what the mind can access. Not because the soul is incapable of knowing more, but because the personality must unfold at a pace that does not overwhelm the emotional body. The soul evolves through emotion — not intellect — and Saturn is the guardian of that process. It creates the conditions where certain experiences cannot be avoided, and certain truths cannot be accessed until the emotional body is ready to absorb their impact.

This is why Saturn correlates to fear, resistance, delay, karma, shame, and responsibility. Not because Saturn punishes — but because it protects. It limits the psyche to a workable range. It slows the soul's expansion to a humane pace. And when Saturn sits in Cancer or the 4th house, that limitation occurs around the deepest, most vulnerable emotional terrain you carry.

Emotional Contract of the Lifetime

Saturn shows you the emotional territory where your soul agreed to grow, stabilize, and mature. This is why Saturn feels heavy: it is the part of you that is underdeveloped and must be built consciously. And it is why Saturn feels non-negotiable: this is not optional evolution. This is required curriculum.

Every Saturn placement tells a story about:
- what emotional muscles you do not yet have

- what you must learn to tolerate
- what part of yourself you avoid because it feels too raw
- where your soul feels least prepared, but most destined, to grow
- what aspects of inner authority must be reclaimed

Saturn teaches through repetition. Through contrast. Through the slow accumulation of emotional capacity. It is the planet that says: "You can learn this — but you will learn it in real time." Saturn does not allow bypassing. You cannot think your way out of Saturn. You cannot manifest your way around Saturn. You cannot avoid the emotional lessons Saturn governs, because Saturn is the structure your soul chose as its foundation. And until the foundation is strong enough, other areas of your chart simply cannot stabilize.

Regulator of Consciousness
Saturn does not only govern physical reality — Saturn governs how much consciousness the physical body can hold. This is why the Saturn return is such a profound turning point. It is not simply an astrological milestone; it is the moment when a soul's architecture becomes mature enough to accommodate higher levels of awareness.

Saturn determines:
- how much truth you can tolerate
- how fast you can awaken
- how much of your spiritual memory you can access
- how much psychic content you can integrate
- how deeply Pluto can take you into your underworld
- how much of Neptune's dissolving you can withstand without shattering

Your evolution is limited not by your desire to grow, but by your capacity to embody. Saturn expands that capacity — slowly, steadily, deliberately — until the foundation becomes strong enough for the soul's deeper curriculum to unfold.

Saturn by sign: the crystallized consciousness
Saturn by sign describes the shape of the stagnation — the emotional template the soul incarnates with, usually formed across many lifetimes. It shows the consciousness that is rigid, pre-structured, and difficult to change without effort. Think of it as the default behavior your soul uses when life becomes too overwhelming.

Saturn in the sign tells you what the soul already knows too well — the part of you that became overdeveloped, rigid, and defended. This rigidity must soften. This structure must be questioned. This consciousness must evolve. Saturn by sign shows the karmic "gravity field" your soul must learn to rework if it is ever going to move into higher states of awareness.

Saturn by House: Where reality refuses to let YOU Bypass

Saturn by house is the area of life that becomes the soul's training ground. It is the room of your chart where growth cannot be postponed — no matter how much you manifest, meditate, or spiritually rationalize your way around it. The house shows the part of your life that feels slow, delayed, blocked, or heavy until the soul's emotional maturity catches up. Saturn's house is the place where each "failure" is actually a structural correction.

The Saturn Return

The Saturn Return is not simply an astrological event. It is the moment your crystallized consciousness becomes too small for your soul's evolution. Between ages 27 and 30, Saturn brings reality into sharp focus. Fantasies collapse. Roles dissolve. Unstable structures fall away. The emotional body is tested, stretched, and confronted with its own limits.

The Saturn Return forces the soul to face three truths:
1. What you have built does not match who you are.
2. The identity you are living no longer serves your evolution.
3. Your soul will not allow you to continue the old path.

This period coincides with the Plutonian exhaustion of separating desires the moment Pluto exhausts the desires that kept you tied to the past. Every soul has unconscious desires that must be burned out before evolution can continue. Some desires must die so others can rise.

Saturn and Pluto work together here:
- Pluto strips the illusions.
- Saturn removes the scaffolding.

This is why the Saturn Return often feels like collapse — because the ego built a life around desires the soul has outgrown.

Esoterically Saturn Form Must be Mastered

In esoteric astrology, Saturn is not the limiter — Saturn is the gatekeeper. It stands between the lower and higher mind. Until Saturn is mastered, the bridge between the personal mind (Mercury) and the universal mind cannot stabilize.

Saturn must be integrated before you can:
- trust your intuition
- access direct knowing
- interpret psychic content without distortion
- stabilize identity-level manifestation
- hold higher frequencies without emotional collapse
- distinguish intuition from trauma
- receive archetypal language without projecting

Saturn represents emotional adulthood — and without emotional adulthood, spiritual awareness becomes fantasy rather than embodiment. This is why many seekers become lost in Neptune fog, Uranian chaos, or Plutonian overwhelm: Saturn was never integrated. Saturn is form.

URANUS
LIBERATION, FREEDOM, DISRUPTION, CHANGE

Uranus marks the part of the psyche that feels raw, exposed, and electrically alive. It is the place where the ego cannot hold its shape, where identity fractures just enough for the truth to break through. Uranus represents the instinct toward liberation — not the gentle, reflective kind, but the kind that arrives suddenly, disruptively, without permission. Where Uranus sits in the chart is where the soul refuses to tolerate stagnation. It is where outdated emotional patterns cannot hold, where old identities collapse, and where life erupts in order to force evolution.

Uranus destabilizes the familiar. It breaks open the places where the ego's strategies are most entrenched. It rips away the illusions that create false safety. It shocks the system awake. The nervous system responds to Uranus with immediacy: adrenaline, intuition spikes, dissociation, flashes of clarity, instinctive rebellion, sudden withdrawal, or the overwhelming need to detach from anything that feels confining. Uranus brings both genius and chaos. Awakening and rupture. Insight and volatility. It is the archetype of the lightning strike — the moment that splits a life into "before" and "after."

Mechanically, Uranus shows where the psyche refuses repetition. It is the part of the chart where cycles do not stick, where routines disintegrate, where life refuses linearity. It exposes the emotional terrain where conformity feels impossible and where authenticity is non-negotiable. Uranus insists on freedom, even when freedom feels like instability. It liberates through disruption when liberation is resisted through fear.

Sign	The sign reveals the nature of the disruptions and the instinctive response the soul learned in order to survive them. Whatever Uranus touches becomes charged with intensity, unpredictability, and a deep unconscious fear of being trapped in the past. The sign Uranus occupies describes the specific behavioral response the nervous system learned in order to survive disruption. This is the pattern that repeats automatically when the past is activated. It is not personality. It is conditioning.
House	Uranus occupies reveals the area of life where this destabilization repeatedly occurs. The house shows where the original disruption occurred or was most impactful, and therefore where the nervous system never learned how to settle. As a result, this life area becomes the stage where the trauma pattern is reenacted again and again. Uranus does not allow this area of life to remain unconscious. If the pattern is avoided, Uranus escalates. If the pattern is repeated, Uranus intensifies. The pressure continues until the system learns how to remain present instead of reenacting the reflex.
Aspects	Pluto → Exposing where trauma-based survival patterns are compulsively repeated until identity undergoes irreversible transformation. Saturn → Forcing awakening through prolonged restriction where freedom cannot be accessed until the nervous system can tolerate stability without collapse. Mars → Reactive urgency, causing impulsive breaks, confrontations, or escapes when unresolved trauma is activated. Moon → The Moon entangles Uranus' awakening function with emotional memory, triggering sudden emotional destabilization when past attachment wounds are reactivated. Mercury → Mercury links Uranus to mental shock, interrupting habitual narratives and belief systems through sudden insight, disruption, or nervous system overload. Venus → liberation with relational rupture, destabilizing attraction patterns so unconscious attachment dynamics cannot continue unchanged. Jupiter → amplifies destabilization, expanding restlessness, belief upheaval, or existential dissatisfaction until growth replaces escape. Neptune → dissolves Uranus' clarity, blurring awakening with

	confusion, dissociation, or spiritual bypass until freedom is grounded rather than imagined.

EXAMPLE

Uranus in the Seventh House of Pisces creates disruption through relationships. Each time a connection deepens, the psyche senses entanglement and instinctively detaches. Pisces absorbs, dissolves, merges. Uranus resists, rejects, pulls away. This combination exhausts the body, destabilizes the emotional field, and pushes the soul repeatedly into dissociation until the underlying wound is recognized. Love is desired, but only when it feels spacious. Connection is craved, but only when it does not threaten autonomy. When attachment begins to form, Uranus triggers withdrawal. When dependency emerges, Uranus shatters it. When fantasy takes hold, reality cracks it open. The soul is forced to awaken to the unconscious patterns of absorption, escapism, idealization, and avoidance that defined earlier relationships.

Uranus in Pisces destabilizes through emotional overwhelm. It shakes the walls of the psyche by flooding it with feeling, then pulling it back into numbness. The exhaustion this creates is not random. It is the soul's way of breaking the trance — of awakening the individual to the unconscious ways they abandon themselves in relationships long before anyone has the chance to abandon them.

The Eleventh House: The Unconscious Grief

The Eleventh House is often described in modern astrology as the realm of community, friendships, networks, visions, and the future. But this interpretation is incomplete. Beneath the surface of its airy themes lies a much older, more esoteric truth: the Eleventh House contains the emotional material the psyche has not been able to process in this lifetime. It is the chamber where ancient grief gathers. It is the psychic reservoir of unresolved memory — not necessarily from childhood, but from the deeper strata of the soul's chronology.

The Eleventh House reveals the parts of you that are emotionally alive yet psychologically unplaced. It is where you feel everything without knowing why. It is where you carry emotions that do not match your present circumstances, reactions that are disproportionate to reality, grief that feels too large for anything you've lived through, and triggers that erupt suddenly, inexplicably, without any linear cause.

This house operates like a fault line. You do not see it until it moves.

But when it moves, the entire emotional field shifts. Feelings surge without context. Longing appears without direction. Sadness arrives without story. The Eleventh House exposes what the conscious mind cannot categorize. It offers no narrative. No linear trail. Only the raw emotional residue the soul has not yet metabolized.

Mechanically, the Eleventh House functions as a psychic echo chamber. It amplifies what has been suppressed. It brings to the surface what no longer fits beneath consciousness. It triggers the deeper emotional imprints in sudden waves — not to destabilize you, but to release what your psyche has carried across lifetimes.

Reading the Eleventh House: Sign, Ruler, and Planets
The sign on the Eleventh House cusp reveals the **emotional tone** of the unprocessed material. It shows how the grief feels in the body, how it expresses itself, and what quality of experience the soul remembers most strongly.

The ruler of the Eleventh House shows **how this grief is activated** and where it seeks resolution. It describes the mechanism through which unconscious memory enters awareness. Any planets placed in the Eleventh House reveal the **density and nature of the imprint**. These planets do not behave casually here. They act as carriers of memory. They sensitize the psyche to specific emotional frequencies and intensify the sense that certain bonds, losses, or longings extend beyond this lifetime.

When the Eleventh House is emphasized, connection is never neutral. Recognition is immediate. Separation can feel devastating. Love can feel ancient. Grief can feel inherited. The ruler of the Eleventh House reveals how this grief expresses itself. The sign on the cusp shows its emotional tone. Any planets inside reveal the density and nature of the unprocessed material.

DISSOLUTION OF THE FALSE SELF

Where Consciousness Remembers It Was Never Separate

Neptune marks the place in the psyche where **form cannot hold**. It is where the ego's boundaries soften, where identity loses coherence, and where the illusion of separateness begins to dissolve. Neptune does not liberate through shock like Uranus. It liberates through **erosion**. Slowly. Invisibly. Relentlessly. Where Neptune sits in the chart is where the soul can no longer sustain a constructed identity. It is where fantasy, longing, spiritualization, and meaning-making emerge not as flaws, but as **transitional states**—attempts to touch something infinite through finite forms. Neptune represents the totality of consciousness pressing against the limits of personality.

The nervous system experiences Neptune as diffusion: fatigue, fog, grief without an object, loss of motivation, dissociation, heightened sensitivity, spiritual longing, and periods of profound emptiness. Unlike Uranus, which spikes the system, Neptune drains it. The body feels unmoored because the reference points that once defined "me" are dissolving. Neptune dismantles illusion not by confrontation, but by **making it untenable**.

The Mechanics of Neptune

Neptune shows where the psyche seeks reunion with something larger than the self—but does not yet know how to hold that reunion without disappearing. It reveals where the ego attempts to replace embodiment with fantasy, devotion, or spiritual purpose when reality feels unbearable.

Neptune dissolves:
- false purpose
- identity-based meaning
- roles built on survival
- desires that were never truly yours

What collapses under Neptune was never real—it was functional.

Sign	The Nature of the Illusion describes how the illusion is shaped—the specific form consciousness uses to avoid the pain of separation. how the soul seeks to dissolve illusion, experience divine connection, and spiritualize its consciousness. This sign colors the style of idealism, dreams, and disillusionment, revealing how the individual may project ultimate meaning onto life experiences. Neptune here spiritualizes the archetype of that sign, but also exposes its shadow through confusion, escapism, or idealization. Over time, the soul learns to transcend egoic expressions of the sign and embody its highest spiritual potential — turning fantasy into vision, and confusion into mystical clarity.

House	Where Identity Must Dissolve: where life refuses to stay solid. This area becomes fluid, unclear, and spiritually charged. Attempts to stabilize it through effort or control fail. This is where the soul is asked to surrender identity, not refine it. Where certainty evaporates. Where the personality cannot anchor itself through familiar roles. Reveals where the soul seeks divine meaning, often experiencing dreams, illusions, or disillusionments. This area of life is where boundaries blur, where the ego dissolves, and where the individual may feel both lost and spiritually called. Surrender, compassion, and a deeper attunement to unseen realities. It's often a place of projection and idealization, but also divine inspiration and higher service.
Aspects	How Dissolution Is Triggered what pulls the illusion apart and how confusion, longing, or awakening is activated. Saturn–Neptune → collapse of rigid structures; spiritual crisis after over-discipline Pluto–Neptune → total annihilation of false identity; existential death/rebirth Uranus–Neptune → awakening through chaos, dissociation, or sudden loss of meaning Moon–Neptune → emotional merging, grief, loss of emotional boundaries Venus–Neptune → romantic illusion, idealization, disillusionment in love

7 EMOTIONAL PATTERNS

This is the emotional blueprint you arrived with — the part of your psyche formed before you had language, memory, or choice. If you want to understand why you react the way you do, why certain wounds follow you from relationship to relationship, why the same inner ache rises even when your outer life looks different, this is the place to look. The ego is not a flaw in the spiritual design. It is not something you are meant to transcend, erase, punish, or view as spiritually inferior. The ego is simply the lens the soul uses to enter form. Without it, consciousness would have no way to localize itself. No way to say "I" instead of "we." No way to experience personal evolution. The ego exists so the infinite can experience itself in a specific, embodied way.

The illusion is not that the ego exists — the illusion is believing the ego is the entirety of who you are. That illusion forms early, long before logic, choice, or memory. Your ego didn't arise from thought; it arose from emotion. It was shaped by the home you grew up in, the nervous system responses you copied, the relational field your caregivers created, the way affection was given or withheld, the way conflict was handled, and the subtle (often unspoken) rules about what parts of you were safe to express. Identity begins as an adaptation, not a conscious decision. The ego is the emotional survival strategy the child needed in order to feel some version of safety.

Astrology captures this with stunning accuracy. The Fourth House reveals the foundation of identity — the emotional soil that produced the ego. The sign on the cusp tells you the kind of emotional environment the child expected. The ruler shows how that environment operated. Any planets inside describe what the child absorbed unconsciously: the atmosphere, the emotional weather, the dominant tone of the home. If the Moon touches this house by aspect or presence, the early imprint becomes even more pronounced. This is the "emotional DNA" of your incarnation.

And then there is the Moon itself — the emotional body. The Moon describes how nurturing was experienced, how emotions were processed, how safety was formed, and what the child had to do to get needs met. It reveals attachment style, early coping mechanisms, and the instincts that become your default responses as an adult. Every Moon sign carries a story. A Moon in Cancer responds differently than a Moon in Capricorn. A Moon in Pisces absorbs environments; a Moon in Virgo organizes them. A Moon in Scorpio trusts nothing at face value; a Moon in Sagittarius searches for meaning inside the chaos. When the Moon is wounded, these instincts become survival strategies. When the Moon heals, they become intuitive gifts.

Children do not interpret their environment — they absorb it. They don't analyze the emotional field; they become it. There is no filter, no discernment, no distance. Whatever the child feels repeatedly becomes the baseline for identity. If the home was unpredictable, the ego learns hypervigilance. If the home was emotionally chaotic, the ego learns to shut down. If love was conditional, the ego learns performance. If safety was inconsistent, the ego learns self-reliance. The ego forms not as a reflection of your true self, but as a reflection of whatever your body had to do to survive childhood reality.

This is why the Moon is not simply the "emotional nature" — it is the blueprint for the ego itself. It is the instinctive self, the conditioned self, the self that reacts before the mind even registers what is happening. These instincts keep repeating until the emotional body integrates what it could not process as a child. The Moon shows the part of you that feels ancient, familiar, reflexive — the part that acts before you think and protects before you understand. It is the conditioned "I" that you mistake for your true self until evolution challenges it.

The Moon is the ego's origin story, written in emotional terms rather than intellectual ones. It tells you how you were shaped, what you internalized, what you rejected, what you learned to expect, what you learned to fear, and what you still carry in your nervous system long after childhood ends. And because astrology is symbolic rather than literal, the Moon shows this not through narrative, but through archetype — through the sign, the house, and the aspects that reveal the emotional architecture your soul chose for this life.

Locating Your Moon and the Emotional Blueprint It Reveals

1. Sign → The Emotional Survival Pattern Your Nervous System Protects

The sign of the Moon describes the instinctive emotional pattern your nervous system learned early and now protects at all costs. This is not a personality trait — it's a survival strategy. The Moon sign shows how you learned to feel safe, how you self-soothe, and how you emotionally stabilize yourself when threatened. The Moon sign reveals: how you react before you think, what emotional states your body associates with safety or danger, how you protect vulnerability, how you unconsciously recreate familiar emotional environments, what you cling to when you feel destabilized, how you emotionally sabotage growth by returning to what feels "known"

Because the Moon governs emotional memory, these patterns are pre-verbal. They live in the body, not the mind. Even when a Moon pattern causes pain, the nervous system resists releasing it — because familiarity feels safer than the unknown.

Every Moon sign has a core emotional need it defends fiercely. These needs are not preferences or wants. They are the conditions your nervous system learned to associate with survival. When these needs feel threatened, the body reacts instantly — through withdrawal, control, emotional flooding, dissociation, caretaking, or defensiveness — long before consciousness can intervene.

2. House → Where Emotional Conditioning Was Formed and Replayed

The house of the Moon shows where emotional conditioning was formed and where it is continuously replayed in real time. This is the life territory where your emotional reflexes are strongest and most automatic. This house is not where you "should" grow — it's where your emotional body already lives. It's where the inner child is still active, alert, and scanning for danger. Because of this, Moon-house experiences feel intensely personal. You don't just experience events there — you *feel* them. When unresolved, the Moon house becomes the stage where the same emotional themes repeat: similar relationships, similar disappointments, similar longings. Evolution here doesn't happen through force or ambition — it happens through emotional safety, attunement, and learning to respond instead of react.

The Moon house reveals: where you feel most emotionally exposed, where you unconsciously seek safety, validation, or containment, where emotional triggers override logic, where you seek comfort or retreat when overwhelmed, where early emotional imprints are re-enacted through people and circumstances.

3. Aspects → What Activates Your Emotional Memory and Triggers Regression

Aspects to the Moon show what activates your emotional memory system and pulls you back into unconscious patterns. These aspects don't create the emotional wound — they expose it. They show which parts of the psyche are wired directly into your nervous system responses.

Pluto → emotional trauma stored in the body, power struggles, fear of emotional annihilation, intensity that overwhelms the nervous system
Saturn → emotional restriction, abandonment fears, emotional self-control, feeling responsible for others' feelings
Mars → fight-or-flight responses, emotional reactivity, anger as protection, impulsive emotional defense
Venus → attachment conditioning, love-equals-safety beliefs, emotional dependency or withholding
Mercury → emotional narratives, internal dialogue that shapes feelings, thinking as a defense against feeling
Neptune → emotional confusion, porous boundaries, emotional idealization, dissociation, spiritualized emotions
Uranus → emotional shocks, instability, sudden detachment, fear of emotional confinement
Jupiter → emotional excess, over-meaning, emotional inflation or avoidance through optimism

4. The Fourth House → The Silent Architect Behind the Moon

The Fourth House is the emotional architecture your Moon was built inside of. Long before you had conscious preferences or choices, the Fourth House environment taught your nervous system what "normal" felt like. This is the backdrop against which your Moon learned how to survive. The sign on the cusp of your Fourth House describes the emotional atmosphere of your early life — not the story that was told, but the felt reality. It shows the tone of the household, the emotional weather, the unspoken rules you absorbed simply by existing there. This is not about whether your caregivers tried, loved you, or had good intentions. The Fourth House doesn't speak in moral language. It speaks in sensation, mood, tension, and safety.

The combination of your Moon sign and your Fourth House sign creates the template for how you learned to survive emotionally. If the Fourth House sign contradicts the Moon sign, the inner conflict becomes even sharper. Imagine a Moon in Pisces — sensitive, porous, dreamy — raised in a Fourth House ruled by Capricorn. You end up with a child who feels everything but learns quickly that feelings are "not allowed," "not practical," or "too much." That child grows up with one emotional need internally and the opposite message externally, and the adult spends decades trying to reconcile those two realities.

The Archetypal Mother

Now gently turn your attention to your mother — not as a person, but as an emotional pattern. The chart does not describe who she "was"; it describes how she lived inside your body. Your Moon shows what she taught you to expect from intimacy. Your Fourth House shows the environment she either created or allowed. If your Moon carries fear, she may have passed down fear. If your Moon carries hypervigilance, she may have been unpredictable or overwhelmed. If your Moon carries self-reliance, she may have been absent or emotionally unavailable. If your Moon carries guilt or performance, she may have needed you to stabilize her. Every Moon holds a mother-story.

Sometimes the Moon reflects a mother who was loving but inconsistent. Sometimes it reflects a mother who was anxious, depressed, chaotic, or absorbed in her own wounds. Sometimes the Moon reflects a mother who was physically present but emotionally unreachable. Sometimes it shows a mother who adored you but demanded too much of your emotional body. Sometimes it shows a mother who tried her best yet still shaped your nervous system in ways you're only beginning to understand.

Your emotional responses today — shutting down, caretaking, absorbing, performing, avoiding, controlling, pleasing, fleeing — are echoes of that original blueprint.

This is not about blame. It is about recognition. When you begin naming the Moon's needs, you begin naming the parts of yourself you've been trying to fix, override, or shame into silence. When you recognize which parts of your emotional nature were supported and which parts were suppressed, you begin to see why your current challenges show up the way they do.

A Moon in Scorpio that grew up in a calm, validating home learns to channel its depth into intuition and insight. A Moon in Scorpio raised in chaos learns to anticipate emotional danger and protect itself with secrecy. Same Moon. Different imprint. Two entirely different lives. Your task is simple, though not always easy:

Look at your Moon and your Fourth House and ask, What did I have to do to feel emotionally safe as a child?
Because whatever that answer is, you are likely still doing it now — and it is running your life more than your conscious beliefs ever could.

When you locate this blueprint, you don't just understand your emotional body — you understand your ego, your patterns, your relationships, your fragilities, your instincts, your triggers, and the unconscious contracts you've been honoring for decades. This is where the true work begins.

How Your Moon Sign Describes Your Inner Emotional Needs

Every Moon sign carries a very specific emotional ecosystem — a subtle but powerful set of needs that must be met for the nervous system to feel safe, grounded, and capable of intimacy. These needs are not "preferences," and they are not weaknesses. They are the energetic conditions your emotional body was designed to thrive in. When these needs are misunderstood or chronically unmet, you don't just feel unhappy — you reenact the same relational patterns over and over again, not because you want to, but because your Moon is trying to find resolution.

The key is knowing what your Moon actually needs, not what the world told you it should need. And the best way to understand that is to translate the emotional logic of your Moon sign into plain human experience.

Below is a universal explanation — adaptable to every Moon sign — that will help you decode your emotional needs with incredible accuracy.

If there is one thing people misunderstand most about themselves, it's this: your emotional body does not respond to general love. It responds to a very specific quality of love — one that matches the emotional imprint you were born with. You can be surrounded by people who claim to love you and still feel profoundly unseen. You can be in relationships that look stable on paper and still feel abandoned inside. You can have friendships, community, and support, yet carry a loneliness that nothing seems to touch. That loneliness doesn't come from lack. It comes from the mismatch between the love your Moon needs and the love you've been taught to accept.

Your Moon sign tells you the precise emotional frequency your nervous system recognizes as safety. It is the original language your emotional body speaks — long before words, long before logic, long before conscious memory. And just like any language, if someone doesn't speak it fluently, you feel the disconnect immediately, even if you can't explain why. Some Moons need tenderness and warmth to feel met. Some need space and intellectual rapport. Some need honesty, even if it's uncomfortable. Some need steadiness, predictability, reliability. Some need depth, intensity, and emotional truth. Others need inspiration, adventure, or spaciousness. None of this is random. None of it is optional. This is the architecture of your emotional reality.

Here's the thing most people never realize: you can't override your Moon. You can override your preferences. You can override your boundaries. You can override your logic. You can override your instincts. But you cannot override the emotional frequency your body responds to. The Moon lives beneath personality. Beneath the roles you play. Beneath even the version of "yourself" you show the world. The Moon is the part of you that decides — without permission — what feels safe, what feels threatening, what feels nourishing, and what feels hollow. It doesn't wait for your mind to catch up. It reacts instantly, whether you want it to or not.

This is why you may find yourself chronically attracted to a certain "type," even though your conscious mind knows it won't end well. Why you may push away people who are good for you while clinging to those who activate your wounds. Why the same relational story repeats, even across different partners, different cities, different decades. Your Moon is searching for a specific emotional signature — not because it's trying to hurt you, but because it is trying to resolve something ancient and unresolved. Emotional patterns are not mental preferences; they are Soul-level agendas.

To understand your Moon sign is to finally understand why certain connections feel like home and others feel like labor. It explains why some people feel comforting from the moment you meet them — even if they barely speak — and why others exhaust you with their presence even when they're being kind. Emotional compatibility is not about matching attachment styles or having similar interests or sharing values. Emotional compatibility is when two nervous systems speak the same language without having to think about it. Your Moon sign describes that language.

Some Moons need closeness to feel safe. For them, distance feels like abandonment. Others need space to feel safe. For them, closeness feels suffocating. Some Moons read love through consistency. Others read love through intensity. Some read love through partnership. Others read love through autonomy. And none of these are wrong. Problems only arise when you expect your Moon to respond to a kind of love it was not built for.

Think of your Moon sign as the emotional "socket" your relationships must plug into. If the plug doesn't fit, the connection doesn't charge — no matter how much effort, communication, therapy, or conscious intention you apply. This is why you can work on yourself endlessly, do shadow work, learn boundaries, meditate, journal, read every spiritual book on the shelf, and still feel stuck emotionally. You are trying to heal a wound without understanding the emotional environment your Moon actually requires to feel safe enough to heal.

When you finally understand the emotional quality your Moon needs — not the one you were raised to tolerate, not the one your partners demanded, not the one your culture idealized, but the one your emotional body recognizes as truth — everything changes. Relationships become clearer. Patterns become coherent. Your triggers make sense. Your attractions make sense. Even your heartbreaks make sense, not as failures but as attempts to resolve a deeper emotional imprint. Your Moon sign does not tell you who you should love. It tells you what love must feel like for it to register as love at all.

And once you know that, you stop trying to fit yourself into emotional environments that were never meant for you. You stop blaming yourself for needs that were wired into your Soul. You stop performing love and start receiving it. Connection becomes nourishment instead of negotiation. And for the first time, you feel what your emotional body has been asking for since the day you were born.

How your relationships with other moons can feel or play out

Archetypally, each Moon expects love to arrive in a specific language. Earth Moons (Taurus, Virgo, Capricorn) feel loved through stability, reliability, and problem-solving. Water Moons (Cancer, Scorpio, Pisces) feel loved through emotional presence, depth, and attunement. Air Moons (Gemini, Libra, Aquarius) need conversation and perspective. Fire Moons (Aries, Leo, Sagittarius) need passion, honesty, and movement. When two people share a similar elemental Moon, their nervous systems tend to "sync" more easily. When they're opposite or very different, the love is still real, but the translations are harder.

Take Pisces Moon and Virgo Moon as a clear example of this. Pisces Moon lives in an emotional ocean — feelings come in waves, often without a clear cause, and the need is to be felt, held, and given space to drift or dissolve. Virgo Moon lives in an emotional workshop — feelings are approached through analysis, practical care, and fixing what's wrong. When Pisces is drowning, Virgo reaches for tools. When Virgo is organizing, Pisces feels even more overwhelmed. Both are trying to care; both can end up feeling rejected. Pisces feels unseen because their feelings are being "handled" instead of witnessed. Virgo feels unappreciated because their efforts never seem to help.

This same pattern plays out with any Moon pairing. A Leo Moon may think, "If you loved me, you'd celebrate me, you'd be excited with me," while a Capricorn Moon thinks, "If you loved me, you'd show up, be responsible, and not make a scene." A Cancer Moon may want long, tender conversations about every emotional shift; an Aquarius Moon may need space and perspective first and only then be ready to talk. No one is wrong. Each Moon is just protecting its own way of staying regulated.

The turning point in any relationship isn't making your Moons identical; it's realizing, "Oh, this is how their Moon feels safe — and this is how mine does." Once you can name that, you stop reading every difference as a lack of love. You can let a Virgo Moon offer practical help without abandoning your Pisces need for softness. You can give a Sagittarius Moon adventure without betraying your Taurus Moon's need for steadiness. The more fluent you become in your partner's Moon, the less you take things personally — and the more your own Moon starts to relax, because it finally feels understood instead of argued with.

8 MIRRORS

The Purpose of Relationship Is the Evolution of the Soul
The purpose of relationship is not companionship, security, marriage, or longevity. Those are external roles. They describe form, not function.
The true purpose of relationship is the **evolution of the soul**. What I learned, often painfully, is that the roles we assign to relationships rarely explain why two souls are drawn together. Marriage, partnership, lover, ex, twin, karmic, soulmate — these labels comfort the mind, but they obscure the real reason connection occurs. Souls do not choose each other to fulfill roles. They choose each other to **activate consciousness**.

I have had relationships that were not soul-bonding in the way people romanticize. I have had connections that formed astrally, not emotionally. I have had relationships that existed only to catalyze collapse, rupture, or awakening. And I have had relationships that stayed longer than they "should have," and others that ended before they ever stabilized. What all of them shared was this: they mirrored something within me that could not evolve in isolation. Some relationships were **astral**, formed through resonance at the level of imagination, projection, or subtle longing rather than embodied intimacy. Some were **catalytic**, designed to break an identity, expose a wound, or force a choice. Some were **transitional**, carrying me between versions of myself. And some were **soul-bonding**, but even those were not about permanence — they were about recognition and memory.
None of them were accidents.

Relationships as Mirrors, Not Fulfillments

The mistake most people make is assuming that the depth of a relationship is measured by how good it feels or how long it lasts. From a soul perspective, depth is measured by **what is revealed**. Every significant relationship mirror:
- how you regulate emotional safety
- how you experience meaning and belief
- how you orient toward the world
- how you merge, resist, or transform

This is why relationships that do not "work" externally can still be profoundly successful internally. They complete their function once the pattern has been seen. The soul does not measure success by happiness. It measures success by **integration**.

The Real Relationship Markers in the Chart
What determines the *purpose* of a relationship is not found in labels like "husband," "wife," or even "soulmate." It is found in the parts of the chart that govern **expansion, safety, orientation, and transformation**.
The most important markers are:
- **Jupiter**, which reveals why a relationship enters your life at all. Jupiter shows what belief, meaning, or worldview is being expanded through connection. Relationships involving strong Jupiter contacts are not about intimacy first — they are about growth. They stretch you beyond who you were before the relationship began.
- **The Moon**, which shows how emotional safety is activated and tested. Moon contacts reveal whether a relationship is regulating, destabilizing, familiar, or re-traumatizing. This is where attachment patterns surface and where the nervous system reveals its truth.
- **The Ascendant and Descendant**, which show how identity and otherness interact. These points reveal what part of the self is seeking reflection, contrast, or completion. Relationships that strongly activate this axis are identity-shaping. You do not leave them the same person.
- **The 8th House**, which reveals the relationship's transformational mandate. When the 8th House is activated, the relationship is not here to be comfortable. It is here to force psychological death, intimacy with truth, and irreversible change. These relationships feel consuming because they are meant to dismantle something that can no longer continue.

These markers tell you **why the soul chose the connection**, not how it should look from the outside.

Why Some Relationships End and Others Evolve
Relationships do not end because love disappears. They end because **consciousness moves**. All relationships operate at the level of the soul first and the personality second. Long before roles like wife, husband, partner, or lover are assumed, souls enter into agreements about growth. These agreements are not about permanence. They are about **evolution**.

Before this life, we agreed to play certain characters in each other's stories. Some agreements were made to nurture. Some to challenge. Some to awaken. Some to break patterns that could not be broken alone. The role itself is never the point. The role is simply the costume consciousness wears to enter the experience.

This is why external labels cannot explain why a relationship ends or continues. You can be married, devoted, committed, or deeply bonded — and still feel an internal pressure to move forward. That pressure is not selfishness or avoidance. It is the soul responding to growth that can no longer be contained in the current relational structure.
When two people evolve at a similar pace, the relationship can transform alongside them. The bond deepens because both nervous systems can integrate what is being revealed.

The relationship becomes a living, adaptive field rather than a fixed identity. But when one person's consciousness expands beyond what the other can meet, tension arises. This is not because one person is "ahead" or "better." It is because the **agreement has reached its limit**. The relationship can no longer serve both souls' evolution simultaneously. At that point, the soul begins to apply pressure.

This pressure may show up as restlessness, dissatisfaction, grief without clear cause, or the sense that something essential is missing. Often, nothing is "wrong" on the surface. The relationship may look stable, functional, even loving. But internally, the soul knows it cannot remain without stagnating. Staying in a relationship where consciousness has stopped expanding requires contraction. It requires the self to become smaller, quieter, less alive. Over time, this creates emotional numbness, resentment, or depression. The soul resists this not out of disloyalty, but out of **self-preservation**.

This is why some relationships end even when there is still care, history, or affection. Their purpose was not to last forever. Their purpose was to **move consciousness to a new threshold**.
Other relationships evolve because both individuals are willing and able to meet that threshold together. The relationship does not stay the same. It sheds skins. It renegotiates form. It releases old roles. But it remains because growth is mutual. From the soul's perspective, neither outcome is failure. An ending means the agreement has been fulfilled. An evolution means the agreement is still alive. What matters is not the role you played in someone's life, but whether the relationship allowed consciousness to expand without betrayal of the self.

How to find your Mirrors in Synastry
Most people discover synastry because they're confused by a relationship. Something feels magnetic, or chaotic, or strangely familiar — and they want answers. "Is this my soulmate?" "Why can't I let them go?" "Why do they trigger me so much?" But synastry is not actually about compatibility. It is about consciousness. It is about what happens inside you when someone else enters your field.

Synastry is the emotional language of two charts colliding — two nervous systems trying to find equilibrium with each other. It reveals the parts of your psyche that were quiet until another person's energy lit them up. It reveals where you feel safe, where you feel controlled, where you feel exposed, and where the old self resurfaces without your permission. Synastry shows how certain people activate parts of you that don't show up on your own chart reading because they only come alive in relationship. It's why someone can make you feel seen for the first time in your life… and why someone else can ignite every wound you thought you'd already healed.

Synastry is the truth behind those mysteries.
And here's the thing most astrologers never explain: someone else's planets do not need to touch any of your planets to affect you. Their planets fall into your houses, and that is enough to shift your entire internal experience. Houses are psychic rooms. They hold memory, desire, fear, and potential. When a person's Mars walks into your 12th house, you feel their fire in your unconscious. When someone's Venus enters your 5th house, you feel awakened creatively or romantically, even if their Venus doesn't aspect a single planet in your chart. When someone's Saturn enters your 1st house, your sense of

identity tightens and strains under their gaze.

This is why synastry reveals the internal impact long before compatibility is even considered. Compatibility asks, "Do we work well together?" Synastry asks, "What does this person teach you about yourself?" Because every relationship — romantic, familial, karmic, brief, lifelong — exposes something essential in you. Something you couldn't see alone. Something your psyche tucked away until the right person walked in.

Synastry shows you:
- why certain people make you anxious for no logical reason
- why you feel oddly vulnerable around someone you just met
- why someone brings out your best qualities instantly
- why someone else brings out your worst
- why a breakup feels like death while another barely stings
- why you repeat the same emotional patterns with different partners
- why certain people are unforgettable, even if the relationship wasn't healthy
- why you feel karmic recognition with some souls and neutrality with others

Synastry is not fate. But it is the map of emotional gravity between two people. And if you've ever felt confused by your reactions to someone — if you've ever wondered why you felt irrationally angry, deeply seen, emotionally suffocated, wildly inspired, or incomprehensibly bonded — synastry gives language to those experiences.

Synastry, when you really understand it, becomes one of the most liberating tools in astrology. Not because it tells you whether a relationship will last, but because it shows you why the relationship exists at all. It gives language to your emotional reactions, your fears, your attraction patterns, your karmic ties, your unhealed wounds, and your deepest growth edges.
It teaches you to stop asking, "Why did this happen to me?" and start asking, "What part of me was activated?" Synastry is the doorway into seeing yourself through the mirror of another soul. And once you understand that, you stop blaming people for triggering you — and you start reading the pattern they came to reveal.

Key Planet Activators in Synastry — Jupiter

If there is one planet in synastry that reveals why someone feels important to your growth, it's Jupiter. People talk about Venus for love, Mars for chemistry, Saturn for karma — but Jupiter is the one that quietly, unmistakably changes your life. Not with intensity, not with crisis, not with karmic heaviness, but with expansion. Jupiter is where you become more of yourself because of another person's presence.

In synastry, Jupiter shows you what you awaken in someone and what they awaken in you. Not accidentally — energetically. Jupiter doesn't need effort or intention. It works the moment two people come into contact. Its presence feels like warmth, truth, possibility, generosity, or clarity, depending on where it lands. We often underestimate Jupiter because its effects are subtle at first. But over time, Jupiter becomes the planet you look back on and say, "That person changed my worldview," or "They helped me see something I would've never seen alone."

Wherever someone's Jupiter falls in your chart, they expand that house. Wherever your Jupiter falls in theirs, you expand that house for them. This is why Jupiter is such a profound activator in relationships — it reveals the precise area where you lift each other out of stagnation or limitation. Jupiter uncovers patterns in ways that feel natural, even when the truth it reveals is uncomfortable.

House it Contacts

Unlike Saturn, which shows where we contract, Jupiter shows where we open. Jupiter doesn't force growth; it invites it. When your Jupiter lands in someone's personal house, your energy naturally gives them permission to grow in that area. And you often won't even notice you're doing it. Something about the way you think, speak, behave, or simply exist creates room in their psyche for expansion.

For example:
- If your Jupiter falls in someone's 1st house, you encourage them to become more themselves. They feel braver, more expressive, more confident around you.
- If your Jupiter touches their 3rd house, you expand their thinking. Conversations with you become catalysts for mental breakthroughs.
- If your Jupiter sits in their 7th, you open them to new ways

- of relating, partnering, and connecting.
- If it falls in their 10th, you push them — gently or dramatically — toward a bigger sense of purpose.

People often remember their "Jupiter people" as mentors, catalysts, or the ones who helped them outgrow their old life.

Jupiter Shows What You Reveal About Someone's Soul Pattern

Jupiter is not just expansion; it is meaning. In synastry, Jupiter reveals the part of you that helps another person interpret their life differently. You help them see the truth behind their patterns, the purpose behind their pain, or the potential behind their limitations.

You may:
- help them understand a repeating relationship pattern
- encourage them to take opportunities they once feared
- show them a worldview they were not raised with
- reveal a belief that has been limiting them for years
- help them trust themselves or life
- inspire them artistically, spiritually, intellectually, or professionally

Jupiter is where you become a guide without intending to. It's where you activate someone's higher path simply by being who you are.

Teacher

When someone's Jupiter touches your chart, something expands in you. You start to see possibilities you couldn't see before. You outgrow roles you thought you were trapped in. You feel encouraged, supported, challenged, or pushed toward your next chapter. Sometimes this expansion is joyful.
Sometimes it feels like being stretched. Sometimes it dismantles a belief you've held for years. But Jupiter never takes away. It reveals more.

The Shadow of Jupiter

Every archetype has a shadow, and Jupiter's shadow is excess. Jupiter in synastry can exaggerate:
- optimism
- risk-taking
- emotional patterns
- beliefs
- fantasies

- blind spots

Sometimes a Jupiter connection makes a relationship feel bigger than it is because the energy amplifies everything — the chemistry, the meaning, the potential. Jupiter can create idealization or inflate certain dynamics until they become unavoidable. It can also magnify the very patterns a person needs to confront in themselves. But even when Jupiter pushes someone too far, it ultimately pushes them toward truth.

Jupiter As Your Soul's Teacher in Synastry
In long-term relationships, Jupiter is often the planet that helps two people evolve together rather than outgrow each other. It's the energy that says, "There's more for you — don't shrink." It keeps the relationship from becoming stale because Jupiter activates growth, perspective, humor, learning, and meaning between two people. Jupiter reminds you that love isn't just about emotional needs or chemistry; it's about becoming more whole through connection.

When you look at synastry through Jupiter's lens, you stop asking, "Why did this relationship happen?" and start asking, "What expanded in me because of them?" Jupiter shows the spiritual utility of the connection — the part of the relationship that made you wiser, clearer, braver, or more aligned with your deeper nature. Because every relationship teaches something.

But Jupiter shows the lesson you actually take with you.

How Each Jupiter Sign Expands You in Synastry
Jupiter sign-to-sign interactions reveal how someone stretches you, challenges you, encourages you, and helps you grow. These descriptions are not about compatibility — they're about expansion. This is how each Jupiter sign pushes you toward the next version of yourself. Use these as archetypal reference points. They describe the style of growth someone brings into your life when their Jupiter touches your chart.

Aries
They ignite boldness in you. They push you to stop waiting, stop overthinking, stop doubting. Their presence urges you to act, initiate, leap, and trust your instincts. Aries Jupiter teaches you the value of self-assertion and the kind of bravery that only comes through experience.

Libra
They expand you through partnership. They push you to understand fairness, compromise, beauty, and the art of relating. Libra Jupiter shows you how to see yourself through another's eyes. They urge you to choose harmony without losing authenticity.

Cancer
They expand you by softening you. They help you return to the parts of yourself that you protect too fiercely. Cancer Jupiter pushes you toward vulnerability, nurturing, and emotional truth. They teach you that safety doesn't come from control but from allowing yourself to be seen.

Capricorn
They push you toward structure, mastery, and commitment. Capricorn Jupiter expands you through discipline and long term vision. They help you become more grounded, strategic, and capable. They teach you that expansion isn't only philosophical — it's built step by step.

Taurus
They slow you down, ground you, and show you the importance of consistency. Their presence encourages you to create comfort, build routines, and commit to what nourishes you. Taurus Jupiter expands you through patience, simplicity, and choosing what actually lasts.

Scorpio
They take you deeper. Much deeper. Jupiter in Scorpio pushes you into emotional excavation, intimacy, power dynamics, psychological truth, and unspoken desires. Their presence forces you to confront what you hide and grow from it. This is the most intense Jupiter placement in synastry.

Leo
They encourage you to shine. They push you to drop modesty and own your gifts, creativity, and presence. Leo Jupiter expands you through celebration, confidence, and visibility. They help you remember the part of you that was born to take up space.

Aquarius
They push you to detach from outdated identities, beliefs, and systems. Aquarius Jupiter expands you through rebellion where rebellion is needed, innovation where life feels stale, and see yourself outside the roles you've inherited. They awaken your inner iconoclast.

Gemini
They wake up your mind. They push you to question everything you assumed was true. They expand your world through options, perspectives, conversations, and new ideas. Gemini Jupiter teaches you that life becomes bigger the moment you become curious.

Sagittarius
They expand your worldview. Pushes you to leave behind small thinking and restrictive beliefs. They urge you to take risks, adventure, study, explore, and trust the meaning behind your experiences. They bring optimism but also confrontation if your worldview is too small.

Virgo
They help you clean up your life. Virgo Jupiter pushes you to develop skill, precision, discernment, and habits that support your growth. They expand you by helping you see what needs to be improved, simplified, or purified. With them, your life becomes more efficient and intentional.

Pisces
They expand you by dissolving the limitations of the mind. Pisces Jupiter pushes you to trust intuition, imagination, spirituality, empathy, and the unseen architecture of life. They help you surrender control and let your life be guided by something larger than logic.

Sphinx: The Fate We Cannot Explain With Logic

There are astrological placements that describe personality. There are placements that describe trauma. There are placements that describe attraction, compatibility, karma, or growth. And then there is Sphinx — the one point in the chart that does not behave like anything else. Sphinx doesn't describe who you are. It reveals what you cannot avoid. It is the symbol of the riddle your soul came to answer — the mysterious gravitational pull you feel toward certain people, places, and timelines that you cannot justify with reason.

When another person's Sphinx touches your chart, the relationship stops feeling optional. It becomes a doorway, a summons, a recognition that bypasses logic entirely. You don't "meet" someone whose Sphinx activates your planets. You remember them.

What Sphinx Represents

Astrologically and archetypally, Sphinx functions like a soul-encoded puzzle: a spiritual riddle, a karmic contract, a destiny point, a doorway your soul already agreed to walk through long before your mind developed preferences. Whereas Pluto pulls you into deep psychological transformation. Sphinx pulls you into fate — not in the fatalistic sense, but in the sense that something in the connection feels pre-written, pre-felt, pre-agreed upon. You don't figure out Sphinx with analysis. It reveals itself through signs, synchronicity, timing, obsession, coincidence, and emotional certainty that makes no logical sense. Sphinx is not romantic by nature, but when it

activates in a romantic relationship, you feel:
- the sense of "I've known you before"
- the impossibility of letting go
- the feeling that this person is tied to your purpose
- the strange magnetism that doesn't match the circumstance

Sphinx is the frequency of divine interference.

Sphinx in Synastry: Why Certain People Change Your Life

When someone's Sphinx touches your Sun, Moon, Venus, Mars, Nodes, or angles, they don't just "influence" you — they awaken something dormant in your psyche. It's as if they trigger a storyline that was waiting behind a locked door. They become the catalyst for a chapter you never would have written alone. Sphinx operates in three primary ways:

1. The Person Who Feels Inevitable Even if the timing is wrong, even if you try to walk away, even if there is no logical reason to continue — you feel pulled back. Not by attachment but by a deeper recognition.

2. The Person Who Unlocks a Hidden Part of Your Soul Something about them reveals a truth about your nature, your purpose, your past-life memory, or your spiritual curriculum. They don't teach you through words; they reveal through presence.

3. The Person Who Forces a Turning Point Relationships marked by Sphinx create irreversible shifts:
    - identity collapses
    - fate-level endings or beginnings
    - a sudden redirect of your life path
    - the completion or activation of karmic contracts

Sphinx is neutral — not benevolent, not cruel. Its only purpose is revelation.

When Your Sphinx Hits Someone Else's Chart

If your Sphinx sits on someone else's planet or angle, you become the mysterious force in their life. You represent a riddle they must solve, a truth they must uncover, or a karmic thread that will not loosen until the lesson completes.

You may feel:
- responsible for them in ways you don't understand

- unable to disconnect emotionally
- magnetized toward their evolution
- strangely important in their soul history

You become an initiator in their storyline — intentionally or not.

Sphinx House Overlays: The Room Where Fate Walks In

When someone's Sphinx falls into one of your houses, that house becomes the stage where destiny shows up in your life. Each house awakens a different type of riddle:

- 1st House: "Why does this person change who I am just by existing?"
- 4th House: "Why do they feel like home or like a memory I can't name?"
- 5th House: "Why does love with them feel creative, fated, or karmically charged?"
- 7th House: "Why do I feel bound to them—even when it's inconvenient?"
- 8th House: "Why does this connection feel ancient, chaotic, or transformative beyond reason?"
- 12th House: "Why do I feel like our souls have met in other lifetimes?"

Sphinx in the 12th or 8th is especially intense. These are the connections that feel spiritual, karmic, unavoidable, or impossible to release.

Why Sphinx Creates Destiny, Purpose, or Chaos

Sphinx does not care about comfort. It cares about meaning.

This is why Sphinx connections often arrive:
- at turning points
- during identity collapse
- when you're ready to shed an old version of yourself
- when your life must pivot in a direction you didn't see coming

Some people feel like a blessing. Some feel like a curse. Most feel like both, depending on which part of your soul they awaken. But the through-line is always the same: Your life is not the same after them. Not because of what they did, but because of what they revealed.

How to Read Sphinx in Synastry

To interpret Sphinx in synastry, look for:
1. Contact with personal planets Sun, Moon, Venus, Mars = fated magnetism.
2. Contact with Nodes This is past-life memory meeting future-life direction.

3. Contact with angles Ascendant, Descendant, IC, MC = major life chapters opening or closing.
4. Contact with Pluto This is where destiny and transformation collide.
5. Where Sphinx sits in each other's houses This tells you the storyline, the karmic setting, the theme of the contract.

Why Sphinx Is the Most Mysterious Point in Astrology

Because you can't "solve" Sphinx. You can only live it. It operates like the myth itself — a riddle you answer through experience, not intellect. Sphinx is the moment your soul whispers: "This is part of your path. You won't understand it yet — but you will." Some connections will stay. Some will leave. Some will pass through your life like a storm or a doorway. But all of them will change you. That is the truth of Sphinx.

9 PUTTING IT TOGETHER

Putting It Together: How a Pattern Comes to Life
When you place a planet into a sign and house, you are watching a living force express itself through a specific unconscious dynamic in a specific area of life.

How Signs, Houses, and Planets Actually Work Together
To understand how a chart operates, you have to stop reading astrology as description and start reading it as dynamics in motion. The chart is not a list of traits. It is a living system. Each component plays a distinct role:
- The sign describes the nature of the unconscious pattern being played out.
- The house describes the arena of life where that pattern unfolds.
- The planet is the living force driving the experience — the instrument through which consciousness moves.
- The aspects describe filters or layers to the experience

When you confuse these roles, astrology becomes abstract. When you understand them clearly, the chart becomes readable in real time.

The Sign: The Pattern You Unconsciously Repeat
The sign describes the quality of behavior and instinct that runs automatically when a pattern is unconscious. It shows how you respond before awareness enters the body. Signs are not personalities. They are behavioral dynamics. For example, Scorpio does not mean "intense" as a trait. Scorpio describes a specific unconscious pattern: survival through emotional vigilance, control through depth, truth-seeking driven by fear of betrayal, repetition of crisis as a way to feel alive or safe

When a planet operates in Scorpio, it will unconsciously express these behaviors until the pattern becomes conscious. The sign shows what kind of game is being played, not who you are as a person. You don't "have" Scorpio. You run Scorpio patterns.

The House: The Stage Where the Pattern Plays Out
The house shows **where in life** the pattern unfolds. If the sign is the script, the house is the stage. A second-house placement doesn't mean "you care about money." It means the pattern expresses itself through:
- survival
- resources
- self-worth
- material stability
- attachment to form

So if Scorpio is in the second house, the unconscious Scorpio pattern — control, vigilance, survival intensity — plays out through money, possessions, security, and value. The same pattern would look completely different in the seventh house (relationships) or the tenth house (career). The house answers one question only: *Where does this pattern repeatedly show up in my life?*

How to Place a Planet Inside an Archetypal Pattern
By now, you understand the archetypes as pattern mechanics, not traits. You know they operate through polarity, tension, and evolutionary pressure. What we do next is place movement inside that structure. That movement is the planet.

A planet is not what you "are." A planet is how an archetypal pattern activates, responds, and evolves inside you.

Most people reverse this. They start with planets and then paste traits onto signs. That approach locks identity in place. We're doing the opposite. We start with the archetypal intention, then observe how a planet behaves when it is operating inside that field. This is the difference between identity astrology and evolutionary astrology.

1. Identify Archetypal Field – Sign
2. Identify Planets Job
3. Combine Archetypal Intention + Planetary Function
4. Place the Pattern in the House
5. Observe Distortion vs. Integration

Step One: Identify the Archetypal Field
Every planet in your chart operates through a sign. That sign is the **archetypal environment** the planet must work within. Do not skip this step. Without it, planets get reduced to personality traits.

Before asking *what* the planet does, ask:
- What is the **core intention** of this archetype?
- What polarity is it trying to balance?
- What does this archetype fear?
- What does it need in order to evolve?

The archetype defines *what kind of lesson* the planet is participating in.

Step Two: Ask What the Planet's Job Is
Every planet has a **function**, not a personality. Planets are not traits you possess. They are **forces of consciousness** with specific jobs to perform inside the archetypal patterns you've already learned to recognize. When a planet is unconscious, its job feels disruptive, painful, or compulsive. When it becomes conscious, the same job becomes evolutionary. So before interpretation, ask one question only:

What job is this planet performing inside this archetypal pattern?
Do not describe the person. Describe the **mechanism**. Use function-based language, not character judgments.
At the most basic level:
- **The Moon** regulates emotional safety and instinctive response
- **Mercury** interprets meaning and constructs reality
- **Venus** bonds, values, attracts, and receives
- **Mars** initiates action, desire, and movement
- **Jupiter** expands belief, meaning, and worldview

And then there are the planets that **do not feel gentle**, because they are not meant to be.

Step Three: Combine Archetypal Intention + Planetary Function
This is where astrology becomes precise and alive. You are not describing a personality trait — you are describing how a force of consciousness (the planet) expresses itself through a particular

archetypal lens (the sign). It's not about what someone *is*, but how energy moves through them. The sign shapes the *style*, the planet reveals the *function*, and together they tell a story in motion.

Step Four: Place the Pattern in the House
Once you understand *what* the planet is doing and *why* it's doing it, the house tells you *where* the pattern repeatedly plays out in your life. The house is not a topic — it's a lived arena of experience. This is where the archetypal lesson is rehearsed through real events, relationships, and circumstances. Patterns don't exist abstractly; they reveal themselves through the same life areas until consciousness enters the scene.

Step Five: Observe Distortion vs. Integration
Every planet expresses in two states: The archetype does not change. The planet's **level of consciousness** does.
- **Distorted** (unconscious, survival-driven)
- **Integrated** (conscious, evolutionary)

Ask:
- What does this planet do when fear is in control?
- What does it do when awareness is present?

Example Moon in Scorpio
Step One: Identify the Archetypal Field
Scorpio is the archetype of transformation through confrontation with what has been avoided, buried, or survived. Its core intention is not destruction, but revelation. Scorpio governs the places where consciousness has fractured through trauma, betrayal, loss, or powerlessness, and where survival strategies were formed in response. This archetype pulls awareness beneath the surface of life, demanding emotional honesty and contact with truth rather than comfort. Scorpio operates where intensity is unavoidable. It senses what is hidden, unresolved, or unspoken, often before anything is visible externally. This sensitivity is both a gift and a challenge. When unconscious, Scorpio equates intensity with truth and believes that safety depends on vigilance, exposure, and control. Crisis becomes familiar. Endings feel inevitable. The nervous system stays alert, prepared for collapse even in moments of stability.

The evolutionary task of Scorpio is to distinguish truth from trauma. Truth instinct arises from present-moment awareness and leads to release, regeneration, and self-directed change. Trauma instinct arises from unresolved emotional memory and drives repetition, obsession, and destructive patterns disguised as transformation. Both feel intense. Only one leads to integration. The polarity of Taurus teaches Scorpio self-reliance and coherence. Taurus shows Scorpio that stability is not a threat and that safety does not require constant dismantling. Through Taurus, Scorpio learns to regulate the nervous system, build inner reliability, and remain present without bracing for loss. Transformation becomes embodied rather than catastrophic.

Step Two: Ask What the Planet's Job Is

The Moon governs the emotional body and the nervous system's instinctive response to life. It is the part of you that reacts before thought forms, before meaning is assigned, before the mind has time to intervene. The Moon determines what feels safe, what feels threatening, and what the body does in response — automatically. The Moon does not operate through logic or belief. It operates through memory stored in sensation. Emotional reactions arise as physical signals: tightening, urgency, heaviness, withdrawal, attachment, pressure to act, or the impulse to protect. These responses are not conscious decisions. They are reflexes shaped by early emotional experience and reinforced over time.

The Moon's function is preservation. It is not concerned with truth, growth, or correctness. It is concerned with maintaining emotional continuity. When something in the present resembles a past emotional state, the Moon responds as if the past is happening again. This is why reactions can feel disproportionate, immediate, and unquestionable. The body is responding to what it recognizes, not what is actually occurring. The Moon is not intuitive by default. It is reactive by design. Until awareness enters the emotional body, its signals feel absolute. Sensation becomes interpretation. Feeling becomes conclusion. Safety becomes urgency. When integrated, the Moon does not stop reacting — it becomes regulated. Emotional signals are felt without being acted upon. Sensation is allowed without becoming story. The Moon's sensitivity remains, but it no longer controls behavior. Its function shifts from automatic survival to conscious emotional presence.

Step Three: Combine Archetypal Intention + Planetary Function

When the Moon operates through Scorpio, the emotional body becomes the primary instrument for survival through truth. The Moon's function is to regulate safety and attachment, while Scorpio's intention is to confront limitation and transmute it. Together, they create an emotional system that is exquisitely sensitive to undercurrents, shifts in energy, and anything that suggests emotional threat or hidden danger.

Early in life, this configuration often forms in environments where safety could be withdrawn without warning. As a result, emotional truth becomes equated with detection. The body learns that survival depends on sensing what is unspoken, anticipating rupture, and identifying threat before it arrives. These strategies are not conscious. Emotional reactions do not arise as thoughts, but as visceral sensations — tightening in the chest, sudden dread, urgency, or an unshakable certainty that something is wrong. The Moon in Scorpio does not pause to evaluate. When triggered, the nervous system activates instantly and past emotional memory floods the present moment. The sensation arrives fully formed, often as a conviction: someone is lying, hiding something, about to leave, or about to cause harm. The intensity of the feeling is mistaken for accuracy. This is not intuition. It is trauma memory moving through the emotional body faster than awareness can intervene.

Because Scorpio governs depth and elimination, the emotional response seeks resolution through exposure, confrontation, or severance. Emotional certainty replaces discernment. The body attempts to regain control by uncovering truth, testing loyalty, or preparing for collapse. As consciousness develops, the evolutionary task becomes regulation before interpretation. When the nervous system stabilizes, the emotional body learns that intensity does not equal truth. Real intuition emerges only after fear settles. Integrated Moon in Scorpio transforms from hypervigilant survival into grounded emotional intelligence — capable of sensing truth without being consumed by it, and of trusting presence without bracing for loss.

Step Four: Place the Pattern in the House
Moon in Scorpio — 7th House
With the Moon in Scorpio placed in the seventh house, the emotional body learns itself through relationship. This is not casual relating. This is where emotional survival, attachment, and safety are forged in direct contact with another person. The seventh house

is the mirror, and with Scorpio here, that mirror reflects intensity, vulnerability, power, and the fear of loss.

Emotional safety is not experienced internally first — it is tested externally, through partnership. The body scans the relational field constantly, attuned to shifts in tone, distance, honesty, and presence. Love feels consuming. Attachment forms quickly and deeply. Bonds are not light; they are visceral, fated, and often overwhelming. The nervous system learns early that closeness carries risk, and that intimacy can just as easily bring devastation as connection.
In lived experience, this placement repeatedly draws relationships that activate old emotional memory. Partners become catalysts, not because they are inherently dangerous, but because the emotional body is wired to detect threat in closeness. Silence feels charged. Neutrality feels unsafe. Distance feels like abandonment. The present moment is easily overtaken by the past, and emotional reactions arrive with urgency and conviction.

The seventh house makes this unavoidable. There is no retreat into isolation long enough to resolve the pattern internally. Life insists on reenactment through partnership. Each relationship becomes a stage where unresolved attachment wounds surface again — not to punish, but to be seen. In distortion, the emotional body mistakes intensity for truth. Fear masquerades as intuition. Control, testing, withdrawal, or emotional confrontation become attempts to restore safety. Relationships feel like emotional battlegrounds, swinging between fusion and rupture.

Step Five: Observe Distortion vs. Integration
In distortion, Moon in Scorpio mistakes trauma-based emotional memory for present truth. The nervous system reacts as if the past is repeating, and emotional certainty replaces discernment. The body believes that reacting immediately will prevent harm, so fear drives interpretation, behavior, and attachment. In integration, the Scorpio Moon understands that its emotional reactions are shaped by past survival experiences and are not automatically accurate reflections of the present. When a reactive pattern arises, the integrated Moon does not suppress the emotion or act on it. Instead, it regulates the nervous system first by grounding in the body and slowing the physiological response. The individual consciously names the moment as a memory response by reminding themselves

that this sensation belongs to the past and that they are safe now. Emotional intensity is allowed to exist without being converted into a conclusion. Only after regulation does clarity return, because truth does not disappear when the nervous system calms, distortion does. The integrated Scorpio Moon learns that intuition becomes reliable only after fear has settled and that real perception emerges from emotional sobriety rather than panic.

Interpreting Your Belief Patterns: Jupiter + Mercury

To understand your belief patterns, turn to the section on Archetypal Patterns (Chapter 6). This is where the language of the planets becomes a map of how your soul interprets the world — not just through action or emotion, but through *thought and meaning-making*.

Belief patterns are most clearly shaped by the interplay between Jupiter and Mercury in your natal chart. Jupiter reveals how you create *big-picture meaning* — your philosophy, optimism, and worldview. Mercury shows how you *process information*, speak, learn, and narrate reality to yourself and others. Together, these two planets shape your inner narrator: what you believe to be true, possible, or necessary.

Ask yourself:
- What stories do I always come back to?
- Do I explain life through hope or fear?
- Is my mind curious or defensive, open or rigid?
- Do I trust what I know — or constantly doubt it?

If Mercury is under tension (hard aspects to Saturn or Pluto), your mental pattern may default to doubt, self-editing, or fear of being misunderstood. If Jupiter is exaggerated or distorted (hard aspects to Neptune or the Moon), you may bypass hard truths or cling to blind faith to avoid pain.

Revisit Chapter 6 and explore how your Mercury and Jupiter archetypes operate. What sign are they in? What house? What aspects do they make? The chart won't just tell you *what* you think — it shows you *why*, and what healing your soul came here to do through the mind.

By naming the pattern, you loosen its hold. The more clearly you see the narrative you've inherited or repeated, the more space you have to choose a different one.

Reframing Beliefs Through Polarity and Integration

Once you've named the beliefs your Jupiter placement has constructed — especially those rooted in illusion, bypass, or inherited ideals — the next step is to deconstruct and reframe them through polarity.

Each archetype contains its own distortion. Its opposite contains the medicine.

For Jupiter in Pisces, the polarity is Virgo — not to correct the dream, but to anchor it into the body, into practice, into life. Pisces receives divine vision. Virgo asks: *Can you live it?* Pisces opens the soul to limitless potential. Virgo reminds the soul that potential means nothing if it never takes shape.

This polarity teaches that belief cannot remain a feeling, a fantasy, or a vibe. It must become a behavior.

Ask yourself:
- Where have my beliefs floated above my life instead of informing how I live?
- What structure would give shape to my deepest knowing?
- How can my body become the ritual ground for integration?

In my case, I had to learn that love wasn't about merging into someone else's field — it was about showing up fully in my own, with boundaries, presence, and discernment. The more I practiced Virgo-level embodiment — nervous system repair, relational accountability, clear communication — the more Jupiter could return to its sacred function: to intuit truth, not escape from it.

The Shadow Self: The Pattern You Can't See
How to Find the Parts You've Disowned

One of the most powerful uses of astrology is identifying your rejected self patterns — the parts of you that were judged, shamed, punished, or exiled early in life. These are the archetypes you've pushed underground — and they now show up through projection, reactivity, or repetition. Take a look at your Chiron placement, as it usually shows up here too.

Step One: Track the Irritation

Start by making a complete list of everything that consistently irritates, triggers, or confuses you. Be specific. What traits in others drive you mad? What kinds of people seem to follow you from job to job, relationship to relationship? What behaviors activate you more than the situation seems to warrant?

For example, maybe no matter where you go, you encounter lazy people. You take on all the responsibility. You resent it. You wonder why no one ever carries their weight. You're always the one who steps up, who leads, who fixes. This isn't random — it's a signal.

Step Two: Find the Archetype
Now connect the irritation to the archetypal quality. You can look up common traits associated with each zodiac sign if needed, or feel your way into it. In this example, the trigger — laziness — is often a shadow trait of Sagittarius (when distorted: unmotivated, avoidant, pleasure-seeking, untethered).
Next: look at your chart. Where do you have Sagittarius? What planet or house does it occupy? Is it intercepted, heavily aspected, or otherwise charged?

Step Three: Recall the Vow
Think about early life. Was there a moment — spoken or unspoken — when you *vowed* to never be like that?
"I'll never be that parent."
"I'll never let myself be weak."
"I'll always prove I'm better than that."
This vow often forms in moments of shame, powerlessness, or emotional survival. The part of you associated with that archetype gets locked away — and you over-identify with its opposite. You perform *only* the "light" side. You become the hard worker, the achiever, the responsible one — not realizing you've disowned a part of yourself in the process.

Step Four: Reclaim the Fragment
The shadow isn't bad. It's just unmetabolized. The goal isn't to become lazy — it's to reclaim the freedom, rest, expansion, or joy that may also live in that archetype. When you integrate the shadow, you stop projecting it onto others and start living from wholeness.

THE UNCONSCIOUS SCRIPT

ASTROLOGICAL LINEAGE & RECOMMENDED READING

This book is an original work grounded in lived experience, nervous-system integration, and direct observation of archetypal patterning. It is not derived from any single source. However, the foundations of **Evolutionary Astrology**, particularly regarding Pluto, the lunar nodes, and soul evolution, were established by the following authors, whose work remains authoritative in this field. Readers seeking a deeper or more classical understanding of Evolutionary Astrology are strongly encouraged to study their work directly, as their work was what helped me understand my soul.

Foundational Works in Evolutionary Astrology
Green, Jeffrey Wolf.
Pluto: The Evolutionary Journey of the Soul.
Seven Paws Press.
A foundational text establishing Pluto as the primary indicator of soul intention, evolutionary pressure, and karmic development across lifetimes.

Green, Jeffrey Wolf.
Pluto: The Soul's Evolution Through Relationships.
Seven Paws Press.
An essential work examining how relationships function as catalysts for soul growth, transformation, and karmic resolution.

Green, Deva.
Relating: An Astrological Guide to Living with Others on a Small Planet.
Seven Paws Press.
A seminal exploration of relationship astrology, emphasizing mirroring, projection, consciousness, and the evolutionary purpose of connection.

www.ingramcontent.com/pod-product-compliance
Lightning Source LLC
Chambersburg PA
CBHW050527170426
43201CB00013B/2109